PRAISE FOR WOMEN WHO \

'I am so thankful for Tamu's book. We are going through a mass awakening when it comes to the way we work and why – and this is the practical guidebook we all need. Let this book comfort and nurture you. Let it also give you a friendly yet powerful shake. I'm so glad it exists.'
EMMA GANNON, JOURNALIST, BROADCASTER, AND *THE SUNDAY TIMES* BEST-SELLING AUTHOR OF *THE MULTI-HYPHEN METHOD*

'This is a timely and loving call-in that myself and countless women need in our world today. Through Tamu's incredibly researched and thoughtfully written observations, a mirror is placed in front of us all asking us to look beyond what society had molded us into, and to reclaim our tenderness. *Women Who Work Too Much* is not another 'self-help' book; it is a defiant act of sisterhood that reminds women that we can undo that which functions to undo us.'
KELECHI OKAFOR, ACTOR, DIRECTOR, AND BEST-SELLING AUTHOR

'*Women Who Work Too Much* asks us to reflect on the toxic systems that have brought us here and offers us a vision for a way forward. Tamu Thomas is a wise and grounded force in the world, creating a space for all of us to exhale and dream a new world into being.'
ASHA FROST, INDIGENOUS MEDICINE WOMAN AND AUTHOR OF *YOU ARE THE MEDICINE*

'By writing this book, Tamu has given women, particularly Black women, an opportunity to truly see themselves and love themselves for who they are, and not for what society wants from them. It is a triumph and a gift of a book to be treasured, shared, and read many, many times.'
RONKE LAWAL, FOUNDER OF ARIATU PR

'This is a truly groundbreaking book – one that I want every woman to have by her bedside table. The moment I opened this book and began reading, I felt a huge sigh of relief. Tamu gets what it is to be trapped in a cycle of productivity, and with love, compassion, and powerful guidance, shows us how we can set ourselves free and finally create realistic lives in which we can thrive.'
SELINA BARKER, AUTHOR, AND CAREER AND LIFE DESIGN COACH

'Tamu takes us from ignoring, minimizing, and pushing through to listening, honoring, and caring for. This book is a tour de force of partnering with the wisdom of your body to live a guided life. With expertise and eloquence, Tamu sings a prayer for the modern woman – and anyone else who needs to hear it.'
NATHAN BLAIR, FOUNDER OF THE SOMATIC SCHOOL

'Affirming and direct; a much needed call to time and body sovereignty, joy, and active rest.'
YRSA DALEY-WARD, AUTHOR, ACTOR, AND SCREENWRITER

'Tamu has such a unique way of recognizing and speaking to the human condition. She understands with such acuity, the constructs, conditioning, and biases that have us all on our hamster wheels ad infinitum. This crucial book – a powerful and insightful combination of joy practice, regenerative self-care, and deep-rooted mindset work – is a manifesto for a different way for women.'
EMINE RUSHTON, HOLISTIC THERAPIST AND AUTHOR OF
AYURVEDA FOR MODERN LIFE AND RECLAIM JOY

'Tamu Thomas does not just advocate for inclusivity, she demonstrates it in the very pages of this book. Rich in tools for any work-addicted woman who feels she doesn't have the time or financial resources for therapy, *Women Who Work Too Much* is your gateway.'
SIMONE HENG, MOTIVATIONAL SPEAKER, AUTHOR, AND HUMAN CONNECTION EXPERT

'Tamu Thomas has crafted an exceptional book that delves deep into the challenges faced by women in a society that often glorifies productivity at the expense of our well-being. We are encouraged to challenge the status quo and create a space where our true worth is not tied to our accomplishments but to our authentic selves. With each turn of the page, we uncover practical tools, empowering advice, and a renewed sense of purpose. So, if you're ready to break free from the shackles of constant busyness and rediscover what truly matters, I wholeheartedly endorse *Women Who Work Too Much*. Let its empowering message guide you toward a life filled with balance, fulfillment, and the liberation you deserve.'
DR. DEBORAH THREADGILL EGERTON, BEST-SELLING
AUTHOR OF *KNOW JUSTICE, KNOW PEACE*

'For too long women have tied our worth to our productivity and it has cost us our sense of selves, our joy, and peace of minds. In this must-read book, Tamu shares her hard-won wisdom for how to unknot yourself from always striving to finally be able to relax into life.'
ZOE BLASKEY, QUALIFIED TRANSFORMATIONAL COACH
AND HOST OF THE *MOTHERKIND* PODCAST

'With *Women Who Work Too Much*, Tamu Thomas has created a landmark of love. This gentle journey achieves with poetic simplicity what seems nearly impossible: a fresh view of how to live well. It's personal, practical, and musical. The threads of her words become, like magic, an inner tapestry of hope and trust. Let Tamu take you by the hand, and come to see the life you are here to lead.'
STEVEN HOSKINSON, FOUNDER OF ORGANIC INTELLIGENCE®

'Passionate, powerful, and practical. A galvanizing call for both inward reflection and a drive towards collective change. It's a movement!'
NICOLA RAE, LIFE AND CAREER COACH

'Tamu Thomas has written a must-read book for our times. It's a prayer answered. In *Women Who Work Too Much*, she addresses the puzzle of why we so often unconsciously choose pain, toxic productivity, and overcommitment when a more loving and fulfilling life is available. To experience that life with added joy, satisfaction, and connection, place this book at the top of your reading list, follow the gentle recovery plan within it, and gift it widely.'

REV. SOFIA LOVE-SCHOCK , RELATIONSHIP TEACHER AND INTERFAITH MINISTER

WOMEN WHO WORK TOO MUCH

BREAK FREE FROM TOXIC PRODUCTIVITY & FIND YOUR JOY

TAMU THOMAS

HAY HOUSE

Carlsbad, California • New York City
London • Sydney • New Delhi

Published in the United Kingdom by:
Hay House UK Ltd, The Sixth Floor, Watson House,
54 Baker Street, London W1U 7BU
Tel: +44 (0)20 3927 7290; Fax: +44 (0)20 3927 7291
www.hayhouse.co.uk

Published in the United States of America by:
Hay House Inc., PO Box 5100, Carlsbad, CA 92018-5100
Tel: (1) 760 431 7695 or (800) 654 5126
Fax: (1) 760 431 6948 or (800) 650 5115; www.hayhouse.com

Published in Australia by:
Hay House Australia Pty Ltd, 18/36 Ralph St, Alexandria NSW 2015
Tel: (61) 2 9669 4299; Fax: (61) 2 9669 4144; www.hayhouse.com.au

Published in India by:
Hay House Publishers India, Muskaan Complex,
Plot No.3, B-2, Vasant Kunj, New Delhi 110 070
Tel: (91) 11 4176 1620; Fax: (91) 11 4176 1630; www.hayhouse.co.in

A catalogue record for this book is available from the British Library.

Tradepaper ISBN: 978-1-4019-7581-4
E-book ISBN: 978-1-83782-076-4
Audiobook ISBN: 978-1-83782-075-7

Interior illustrations: © Tamu Thomas

10 9 8 7 6 5 4 3 2 1

Printed in the United States of America

This product uses papers sourced from responsibly managed forests. For
more information, see www.hayhouse.com.

*Dedicated to my daughter Zia, the one I have to
cherish, my most profound teacher and guide.*

*In honor of my granddad Rufai Moses Richardson
Thomas: Thank you for being by my side.*

*With gratitude to my Good Grandmothers:
Your guidance lives in me.*

*To my inspirational Mum: Thank you for
always being my biggest cheerleader.*

Mus and Vanessa: You are the wisest big little siblings ever.

Dad: Thank you for handing me the baton.

CONTENTS

Dear One,

You are powerful.

And it's time to treat yourself that way.

It's time to grow into your true potential,
not an arbitrary idea of 'success.'

It's time to listen to the wisdom of your body
as it provides guidance about what you need
in order to please yourself – yes, really!

It's time to trust your inner knowing, to go at your
own pace, and to be an advocate for yourself, so that
you connect with others without people-pleasing.

INTRODUCTION

We have forgotten that we are miracles made of stardust. We've become so bogged down with performance that we don't know who we are and whose we are. We've forgotten that we share DNA with flora, fauna, and much of the animal kingdom – an embodied reminder that we are all inextricably linked. From the towering baobab tree to the majestic elephant, the delicate daisy to the newborn's first breath, we're all wondrous creations shaped by evolution and experience. And yet, we have allowed our preoccupation with success to stunt our growth.

We've been conditioned to treat ourselves like commodities, constantly extracting from our finite resources of time, energy, and emotional capacity in the hope that we will get a sense of worth, purpose, value, and community – the things that give our life meaning. Productivity is the new religion; success has become our salvation. And if, in salvation, we find deliverance from sin, then what is our sin? To be deemed lazy and unproductive.

Toxic productivity is the unconscious, obsessive-compulsive desire to be productive *all the time*. It's when you build your life around work and forget the purpose of work is to make a living in order to live. It's the process of being detached from the present and focusing on the future. A future that holds the promise that 'one day' you'll have worked enough and achieved enough success to feel fulfilled and worthy enough to enjoy your life. We are taught that success is the result of hard work, and this message is woven into our system of patriarchal capitalism that teaches us to base our value on what we produce, not who we are.

And yet, somehow, this pursuit of success feels unsatisfactory, because it's based on untruths that have been constructed to keep us in pursuit of a target that is always so tantalizingly out of reach. Chasing success destroys the awe and wonder of life, boxing us into the uppermost parts of our heads as we make decisions that override our innate intelligence – and call it logic!

We've forgotten that we are living, breathing, beautiful, sophisticated organisms with legitimate needs that remind us just how precious we are. We've been conditioned to believe that time and space must be occupied with immediately tangible outcomes, even though those outcomes are set up for us to internalize a pervasive sense of inadequacy. And so, we've forgotten that we need space to *be* in our pursuit of doing.

We've forgotten what it is to live in harmony with the wisdom of our bodies. We've been socialized to believe that we cannot trust ourselves and our rhythms. But we are beginning to remember. It's clear in endeavors like the tracking of our menstrual cycles and openly embracing life's transitions – from candid conversations on perimenopause* to petitioning parliament for better childcare provisions. We are slowly repairing the rupture in our relationships with ourselves, caused by a relentless drive for us to use time efficiently. This culture of urgency was forced into a pause by the

---

* Although the word 'perimenopause' still comes up as 'unfound' in my computer program's spellcheck!

catastrophic events of 2020, which caused many of us to begin to finally listen to our bodies telling us it doesn't have to be like this.

One sunny day in September 2017, I woke up with a pressure headache and throbbing pain in my sinuses. As I opened my eyes, I realized my head felt heavy, my neck stiff, and my jaw tight, indicating that I must have been bracing myself as I slept. This is one way my body tells me I'm feeling anxious. Anxiety is our body's way of communicating real or perceived terror. I'd had this headache and stiffness for so long that I accepted it as a normal part of being a mother and a professional. I'd normalized sensations of terror, and pushing through these symptoms was perceived by those around me as a strength – I was often praised for it.

I slept with my curtains open as I love the way the morning light wakes me gently. Waking up to the robotic sound of an alarm was too startling for my frazzled nervous system. I lay in bed for a moment, looking at the blue sky and hazy sunshine. I was comforted for a few seconds until I got distracted by brain fog that felt like tightly stuffed cotton wool pressing against the circumference of my head and extending to my jaw.

I considered taking painkillers but decided I could manage the dull, throbbing pain. This was not unusual. For the past decade, this had been my morning routine: dismissing my body's signals and its needs so that I could be productive – one of the many ways I consciously embodied the 'strong Black woman' stereotype. I'd learned that attending to essential needs equaled me being far too needy, and the antidote was to squash these down with will, discipline, consistency, and strength.

As I sat up that morning, I was greeted by the familiar sinking feelings of dread and panic. My insides felt like cogs spinning rapidly and my body felt like a container keeping it all together. My brain started its usual practice of overthinking and catastrophizing as I ruminated on my work, wondering if it and, therefore, if I was good enough. I didn't know at the time, but overthinking was a coping strategy I used (with great skill) to avoid feeling my feelings.

That morning, things were exacerbated because I had to give expert evidence in a contentious court case. I was a social worker and giving evidence in court was a standard part of my job. In fact, I was very good at it. I told myself I wasn't fazed and reminded myself that I'm a badass and my recommendations were balanced and fair.

I mentally ran through all the things that could possibly go wrong and imagined all the ways I could 'prove' that I was professional if the worst happened. For me, the worst was being told that I'd made a mistake and/or I hadn't worked hard enough. As far as I was concerned, a criticism of my work ethic was a criticism of my character and my worth.

My ability to imagine the worst-case scenario had served me well in my career. This hypervigilance meant that I was always prepared, that I overworked to cover all my bases, to minimize unconscious bias, and avoid criticism by making myself 'convenient.' As a woman, being inconvenient makes you 'difficult' – and difficult women are celebrated for their success while being ostracized for their 'personalities.' As a dark-skinned Black African woman at the intersection of discrimination based on my gender and race, being difficult is something I learned to circumvent because of the racialized stereotype that portrayed us as being aggressive. This is an outcome of what I refer to as the 'oppressive trinity' of white supremacy, patriarchy, and capitalism.

Hypervigilance is an intergenerational ability that I have inherited from my parents, elders, and ancestors. It comes via changed genes (more about this later), which makes it appear to be second nature. This skill helped me know when I needed to protect myself by code-switching, intellectualizing, using humor, or making myself smaller.

Hypervigilance has its advantages, but the downside far outweighs the benefits. For example, overworking suspends you in a perpetual state of 'not-enoughness' that ravages your *life-force* energy. This is not an individual issue. It's systemic. Our systems are designed to keep us striving but never realizing, consuming our way out of feeling and commodifying ourselves so that we may continue to consume. In my case, consumption was no longer an option. Consuming praise, courses, books, and strategies was not enough to silence the signals from my body asking me to care for *me*. External validation began to feel akin to eating a bar of chocolate to satisfy a craving when what I really needed was a wholesome, home-cooked meal.

Nevertheless, on that day I set off for court; I had to be professional and keep it together, heart palpitations or not. On the Tube, I could feel myself getting hotter and hotter. On the escalator, I began to feel faint and could feel my hands becoming clammy. As I left the station, my heart was pounding against my chest, and I could hear my heartbeat in my ears. My mouth was dry and suddenly, I felt as if my knees had disappeared. For a moment I wondered if I should call an ambulance, but quickly told myself that would be ridiculous. I managed to get to a bus stop and hold on to it, forehead dripping with sweat, my neatly styled hair starting to shrink at the roots. I felt as if I'd forgotten how to exhale.

I was dressed in a smart pencil skirt and fitted blazer. My shoes were polished, and my black leather bag said I was a professional person doing professional-person things, yet here I was holding on to the bus stop looking as if I'd taken LSD. People looked at me quizzically, not sure what to do or say to the well-dressed woman who looked like she was on a bad trip.

I did some deep breathing and focused on elongating my exhale. As my breath began to settle, I remembered to focus on my senses and asked myself what I could see, smell, touch, taste, and hear. I somehow managed to get to court and give expert evidence. I was relieved that I hadn't let anyone down and my professionalism had been praised but my memories of the rest of that day remain a blur.

The next day I made an appointment to see my GP. She offered me anti-anxiety medication and a referral for Cognitive Behavioral Therapy (CBT), as my symptoms pointed to 'severe-moderate' depression and anxiety. At a follow-up appointment, blood-test results showed I had very low levels of vitamin D and neutrophils, a type of white blood cell that's vital for immune system health. This explained why I had colds for six months of the year and was constantly low in energy. I had a telephone consultation with a psychologist who told me that what I was referring to as periods of heightened anxiety – like that day on my way to court – were, in fact, panic attacks.

Finally, I had the wake-up call that was too loud to ignore. My focus on being useful, productive, and convenient had made me a stranger to myself. I decided I needed to befriend myself and begin the journey of weaving all my scattered parts back together so that I could experience myself as whole.

And so, the reintroduction to myself began. I saw a nutritionist. I started having coaching. I started reading and listening to podcasts. As I learned more, I began to understand why I'd neglected myself so badly. I saw that I believed being successful would give me the right to meet my needs. I'd learned that self-care had to be earned. My conditioning meant that I hadn't learned how to cultivate self-trust, so I didn't believe my body's signals. For example, I couldn't admit to actual exhaustion, it had to be that I lacked discipline. As such, slowing down and looking inside felt unsafe.

Blaming myself instead of the system in which we live was the safer option, as I could control myself but I was powerless against a system built for my oppression. Instead, I focused on what I knew I could control: working hard and getting the temporary reward of external validation. Sound familiar?

Once I saw my pattern of toxic productivity, everything fell into place. Then I began to see it reflected everywhere, like a disco ball of mirrors. I saw it in my family, friends, colleagues, on TV, and all over social media. It feels like you're living in a pressure cooker and the whistle is starting to blow. As the pressure increases, so does the whistle. The pressure feels so intense that you become scared of what's inside, so you distract yourself by being busy because you've never really learned how to show yourself care. This realization left me feeling bereft and angry enough to know I needed to act.

Like me, you might have turned to self-improvement and hoped the answers would be found if you could just break through your limiting beliefs and improve your self-worth by working on your mindset. In other words, if you could experience a transformation and become a different, more worthy person. I was going to be someone brand new until I finally realized that what I needed was to be *me*. To feel safe enough to connect with all that I was feeling, to stop covering over the cracks with productivity, and – finally – to allow myself to be powerful.

In an industry full of books with hacks and how-tos, I want this book to be an oasis that offers you an opportunity to see yourself beyond your role and titles. It will give context to how you learned to neglect yourself and provide practices to support you to become your own best friend.

Women Who Work Too Much dives heart-first into the roots of a culture that glorifies relentless productivity, leaving women feeling overwhelmed, burned-out, and disconnected from our true selves. Let's face it: our patriarchal, capitalist culture has a lot to answer for. It has normalized the idea that our worth is directly tied to how much we accomplish and how busy we appear. But in this journey of self-discovery and liberation, we challenge these societal norms and create a space for radical change.

Women Who Work Too Much is not just about finding work–life balance; it's about uncovering the deep-rooted fears and insecurities that drive our need to constantly prove ourselves. We will explore the emotional and psychological factors that keep us trapped in the never-ending cycle of productivity. Enough is enough.

This is not your typical self-help book. No, this is a soulful exploration of self-care, connection, and social justice. *Women Who Work Too Much* digs deep into the intersections of race and gender, acknowledging the unique challenges faced by women of color within this toxic-productivity culture. Our journey toward liberation must include an unwavering commitment to dismantling systems of oppression.

Throughout this book, you'll be guided through practical, nervous-system-friendly strategies. We'll explore the art of setting healthy boundaries, cultivating self-trust, and nourishing your nervous system. These practices are not just luxuries; they are vital tools on your path to reclaiming your life and experiencing the joy you deserve.

Compassion, connection, and kindness are at the core of our mission. You are invited to embrace self-compassion, to foster deep connections with others, and to cultivate a kinder relationship with the planet. These are not utopian ideals; they are tangible actions that can transform your life and the world around you.

I know it won't be easy – it is indeed a challenge. Society will continue to pressurize you to perform, to achieve, and to conform. But together, armed with the wisdom and guidance in this book, we can create a ripple effect of change. We can challenge the status quo, redefine success on our own terms, and find true fulfillment.

So, are you ready? Ready to break free from the shackles of toxic productivity? Ready to reclaim your power, your joy, and your life? Then let's embark on this journey together. Let's create a world where women thrive and where self-care and social justice walk hand in hand. It all starts with you, dear one. Let's dive in.

Dear One,

May you wake up, stand tall, gaze unflinchingly at
yourself, and declare, 'Today I prioritize what I need
to do – the everyday essentials that open me
up to what I really want, rather than the life
I have been conditioned to settle for.'

And so it is.

CHAPTER I

HOW DID WE GET HERE?

'Men often ask me, "Why are your female characters so paranoid?" It's not paranoia. It's recognition of their situation.'

Margaret Atwood

I t's not your fault.

I'm very mindful of the words I use. Words shape the way we see ourselves, our environment, and the world. Words carry meaning and the meaning we assign gives them great power, which can create or destroy. In a late-stage capitalist, patriarchal society that generally uses power to dominate, many of the words we use day to day can be disempowering. Many of the words we use are more suited to machines made of metal and plastic, powered by fossil fuels, than they are to human beings with needs, cycles, organs, and nervous systems that inform who we are through the passage of time.

Words such as 'fault,' 'discipline,' 'consistent,' 'productive,' and 'efficient,' for example, are often used in inhumane ways that do not honor the awe and wonder of ourselves as complex ecosystems within a complex ecosystem. When I consider the meaning of these words and their origins, my body contracts and I brace myself as I prepare to squeeze into the confines of meanings that have no respect for human nature. The weight and rigidity of these words force us to make our humanity smaller, shoving it into the nooks and crannies of life. This is reflected in our bodies as we sharply inhale, then shallow-breathe as we embark upon being more disciplined, or when we live in a constant state of fast-forward in the name of efficiency. Few people feel spaciousness and flow when they think about words such as 'consistent' and 'productive.' In fact, these words tend to make us feel unsafe, as we use them to dominate who we are with and/or who we think we *should* be.

The words 'fault,' 'discipline,' 'consistent,' 'productive,' and 'efficient' are commonly used in relation to work, whether paid or unpaid. For a moment, I invite you to look at the meanings of these words:

- **Fault:** An unattractive or unsatisfactory feature, especially in a piece of work or in a person's character.

- **Discipline:** The practice of training people to obey rules or a code of behavior using punishment to correct disobedience.

- **Consistent:** Always behaving or happening in a similar, especially positive, way. The adjective means 'not changing.'

- **Productive:** Producing or able to produce large amounts of goods, crops, or other commodities.

- **Efficient:** A system or machine achieving maximum productivity with minimum wasted effort or expense.

I share these words not because I believe words must always be positive – that would be naive of me. I share them because we all use these words with such frequency that our minds have detached from their origins – but our bodies remember (or 'keep the score').[1] Our bodies remind us with sensations and signals that tell us we are under threat. These sensations impact us, whether we are able to detect them or not.

I try not to use these words in relation to people, but so much of the personal development and self-help world frames our challenges as an individual issue as opposed to a systemic problem. We are told we manifest our reality; we need to think positive, be more disciplined and consistent. This focus on the individual distracts us from the symbiotic nature of humanity and how our environment impacts us. We often make the mistake of blaming and shaming ourselves, or taking responsibility for not fitting into environments that were designed to keep us out or keep us small. For example, at an event I hosted called Indigo Monday, an event to challenge the notion of Blue Monday, I led a workshop called 'Be Your Nervous System's Best Friend' (more about this later). I taught my guests about the different branches of the autonomic nervous system and asked them to reflect on what triggers their survival responses (the automatic fight, flight, freeze, or fawn reactions we all have when we perceive we are in danger or under threat; *see page 47)*. When I spoke about the 'fawn' survival response, where a person people-pleases to reduce or avoid conflict, one of my guests immediately identified that this is something she does as an autonomic (automatic) reaction to racial microaggressions at work.

This highly qualified, intelligent, and charismatic woman learned to protect herself from racism by appeasing the people and institution causing her harm, as though her identity was at fault. Consciously, she knows this makes no sense but in an environment that makes her feel like she is 'wrong,' her need to survive overrides logic.

> *'The brain can become addicted to productivity just as it can to more familiar sources of addiction, such as drugs, gambling, eating, or shopping. A person might crave the recognition their work gives them, or the salary increases they get. The problem is that just like all addictions, over time a person needs more and more to be satisfied and then it starts to work against you. Withdrawal symptoms include increased anxiety, depression, and fear. [Work is] seen as a good thing: the more you work, the better. Many people don't realize the harm it causes until a divorce occurs and a family is broken apart, or the toll it takes on mental health.'*

**Dr. Sandra Chapman, Director of the Dallas Center
for Brain Health at the University of Texas**

WHAT ARE THE ORIGINS OF YOUR TOXIC PRODUCTIVITY?

Dr. Gabor Maté, a Canadian physician and author with a special interest in childhood development and trauma, has written and spoken extensively about the connection between early childhood experiences and addiction, including work addiction.[2] Dr. Maté emphasizes that work addiction isn't simply a matter of individual choice or willpower. Working too much is a complex issue that has been woven into the fabric of our society. It's systemic; therefore addressing work addiction requires a holistic and compassionate approach that considers your early childhood experiences, your current social and emotional context, and the broader societal factors that contribute to the culture of overwork and burnout.

From the moment we enter school at four or five years old, we're conditioned to design our lives around work. As such, this pattern is normalized and children who struggle to manage their natural impulses and curiosity are often perceived as not conforming to what is deemed 'normal.' Our education system conditions us to believe that anything other than spending five days out of seven working for most of your waking day should be considered less-than, lazy, inadequate.

Our earliest years are spent with our caregivers teaching us what our human needs are and how it feels to have them met. As we begin to develop the ability to meet our needs and demonstrate a degree of independence we are moved on to the next phase of our development: subdue, control, and manipulate. This is the phase when we are taught that our innate human needs are an inconvenience and we set about perfecting the skill of self-abandonment in exchange for being 'convenient' and 'productive.' When we are hurt, we are told not to cry, to be brave, and our pain is minimized or denied. As we swallow down primal sounds and hold onto our tears, we are rewarded with praise – four simple words woven together to create a sentence that is intended to be loving but in this situation is embodied as stifling: 'There's a good girl.' And who doesn't want to have the coveted title of being 'good'? Consequently, we learn that pain must be suppressed if we are to be good, and bravery is promoted over empathy. As we grow up, this evolves into profit over humanity. This creates a pattern of trying to be fearless, or adopting the equally dangerous practice of squashing feelings down and pushing through pain when what is really required is the expansive life skill of self-compassion.

Much of our conditioning makes us ashamed of who we are. Many of us experienced caregivers who unwittingly used shame as a means of discipline; using phrases such as, 'You should be ashamed of yourself,' and 'I'm so disappointed.' If you've used these phrases to address children, please do not be ashamed. This is not a covert attempt at shaming you! In the past, I've used the phrase 'I'm disappointed' as a means of correcting my daughter's behavior. I'll even confess to adding the word 'so' for emphasis – 'I'm *so* disappointed' – because I knew it would make her stop and think. However, at the time I didn't realize this could cause her to feel shame; I didn't understand the impact of shame. I believed it to be a motivational tool.

So, we adapt and develop coping strategies to manage the feelings of shame caused by our conditioning. This adaptation serves us well as children and in our youth but becomes maladaptive in adulthood, because shame prevents us from being able to hold the level of vulnerability necessary for us to embrace our authentic selves and form authentic connections. It traps us in a cycle of self-doubt and self-criticism, inhibiting personal growth and prioritizing the illusion of perfection over progress. This hinders us from forming a healthy, respectful relationship with ourselves, or mutually respectful relationships with others and our planet. Over time, this can lead to feelings of inadequacy and dissatisfaction and a pervasive sense of malaise that becomes normalized.

This conditioning creates an unconscious pattern of the pursuit of external validation to lessen the feelings of shame and inadequacy – but it's impossible. External validation is a moving target. It's never enough and this cycle will keep you trapped in a pattern of 'not-enoughness.'

That is, until you show yourself that you're worthy by treating yourself as such.

TOXIC PRODUCTIVITY AND ME

Where did my own toxic-productivity conditioning come from and how did it impact the identity I formed? It's important to note the various parts that came together to create my experience. I'm one person, one organism in our complex ecosystem. I can't and don't speak for all individual Black people, nor do I wish to – we are not a monolith. Similarly, I can't and don't speak for all individual women. However, it is likely that you'll identify with parts of what I share because we are all human beings with a nervous system, vital organs, skin, bone, and flesh.

I am first-generation British of African descent. I identify more as a Londoner than British due to the 'othering' I experience outside the M25 motorway. I was raised in a multi-faith household, which is normal in my parents' homeland of Sierra Leone. I knew that we were different – graffiti saying things like 'Ain't no black in the Union Jack'[3] and one of my white friends at school telling me she wished I were white made that abundantly clear. I couldn't (and still don't) understand why people thought 'different' was bad. The perception of our difference as something 'bad' naturally led people of color to bond, due to the trauma of our shared oppression and our desperate desire to escape it. I was raised by Pan-African activists who engaged in emphatic discourse about equality while upholding patriarchal standards – with my mother working, studying, and taking care of all the domestic and emotional labor in the household. My parents were revolutionary in thought but survived discrimination at work by assimilating with the autonomic 'fawn' response many people of color default to as a means of protection (more about 'fawn' in Chapter 2).

My mother was my first example of toxic productivity – she was a woman who worked too much. I saw this pattern reflected in the women around me. As a child, I didn't know that this was a means of survival, so it became my norm. Over the years, I saw the way women's unrelenting productivity turned into qualifications and promotions that paved the way for mortgaged houses, nicer cars, and trips 'back home' for leisure – not just for funerals or issues with property or land.

The overarching message was that working hard was a panacea for all ills and that as a Black person, I would have to work twice as hard for the same recognition as my white counterparts. And as a Black woman, I would need to behave a certain way and not associate with 'those Black girls' to avoid the 'angry Black woman' stereotype.

As for rest, sleep after a hard day's work was rest. Anything more than that was considered 'lazy' and being lazy was 'useless' and uselessness was a source of deep shame. In fact, 'useless' was one of the most insulting words reserved for arguments and gossip. From a very young age, I understood that working hard all the time would lead to success one day and after that, I could retire and enjoy my life.

However, my Aunty Aminatta did not fit the status quo. She was an international businesswoman. She traveled all around the world which was (and still is) a huge deal for a woman living in Sierra Leone in the 1980s. She spoke several languages and worked for organizations such as the United Nations. When she came to London, she would stay with us or at a luxurious flat in Baker Street. She always looked so jolly in her pencil skirt suits, Flori Roberts makeup, and the bounciest Jheri curls. The way people talked about Aunty Aminatta made it clear that she was someone they respected and, to a degree, admired. As far as I knew, Aunty Aminatta did not look like her work took everything from her, leaving her with the dregs of her life. She looked like she was *full* of herself rather than selfless. I remember looking at her when I was about six years old and thinking, *I want to be an international businesswoman, too!*

Sadly, I forgot about being an international businesswoman because I was surrounded by people working tirelessly to create a better life for themselves, their children, and relatives back home who looked forward to barrels of international goods and envelopes of cash when someone was traveling.

I also experienced the way my mother would prepare when we were having company. No skirting board, door, frame, or handle was left untouched. Heaven forbid if someone visiting saw evidence that humans actually lived comfortably in their own homes! Jokes aside, the lesson I learned is that presentation and, furthermore, people's *perception* of your presentation is all important.

Although I saw people obtain material goods and assets that indicated success, the pattern of survival continued.

The overarching messages I learned were as follows:

- Success makes you important.

- Hard work gives you status, but your status will never alleviate discrimination – it just makes it more covert.

- Work takes everything and you get what's left.

- There is no time to enjoy the fruits.

- Rest is for retirement.

- As a Black woman, I have to work twice as hard to be seen as equal to my white counterparts, but I'll never actually be equal.

'The greatest damage done by neglect, trauma or emotional loss is not the immediate pain they inflict but the long-term distortions they induce in the way a developing child will continue to interpret the world and her situation in it. All too often these ill-conditioned implicit beliefs become self-fulfilling prophecies in our lives. We create meanings from our unconscious interpretation of early events, and then we forge our present experiences from the meaning we've created. Unwittingly, we write the story of our future from narratives based on the past....'

Gabor Maté

Journal Prompts

Here are some journal prompts to help you identify the origins of your beliefs around success and productivity (write whatever comes to mind – there is no 'right' answer, and your responses don't need to make 'sense'):

- In relation to rest, what was role-modeled to you in childhood?

- What are your earliest memories of grown-ups and work?

- When you were a child, who did you consider as successful and what made them a success?

- What were you consciously and unconsciously taught about doing well?

- If you're a person of color, what did you learn about the impact the color of your skin could have on your success?

- What did you learn about being a successful woman at work?

Re-read your responses. What is coming up for you? Are you experiencing any sensations in your body in response to these prompts and your reaction? If you feel numb, don't worry. Feeling numb *is* feeling! Ask the sensation what it wants you to know. This may sound weird, but our sensations often hold our deepest truths and oldest memories.

If this feels overwhelming or brings up a painful memory, I invite you to pay attention to whatever you're sitting, standing, or lying on. Feel where your body makes contact with the surface beneath you. Then look around you so that you become aware of where you are in this moment. Then turn your attention to your breath and see if you can inhale a little more slowly and exhale a little longer. Look at your phone, watch, or something that will remind you of the time and date. This will help you to connect with the safety of the present, so you do not relive an experience from the past.

Ujjayi Breath

A practical exercise to support you to begin to release anything this brings up for you is Ujjayi breath. This is a breathing technique used in yoga. It involves slightly tightening the back of your throat to produce a gentle 'hhaaaa' sound when exhaling. The practice of Ujjayi is said to help calm the mind and regulate the breath, which is good for stress relief. This is a practice and, as such, you need to do it regularly to benefit. I recommend practicing this technique first thing in the morning and when you're feeling stressed.

1. Sit comfortably with a straight back and close your eyes.

2. Breathe in deeply and slowly through your nose. As you inhale, let your chest fill with air until your stomach starts to expand. Be gentle. As soon as you start to strain it's time to exhale.

3. As you exhale, make a soft 'hhaaaa' sound and gently contract the muscles in the back of your throat.

4. The exhale should be slow and controlled, and the sound should be similar to the sound you hear when you hold a seashell to your ear.

5. Repeat this pattern of breathing for a few minutes, focusing on the sound and sensation of the breath.

6. Remember to breathe from your stomach and not just your chest. The goal is to make a smooth, continuous sound with each inhale and exhale. Ujjayi breath is used in many styles of yoga to help focus the mind and calm the nervous system.

I love Ujjayi breath. It allows me to 'let out my wild' and remember that I'm a mammal without overwhelming me.

////////////////////////////////////

THE CONSEQUENCES OF LIVING TO WORK

The way we overwork and under-live negatively impacts our ability to function, the choices we make, and our health. Over time this is traumatic. You need to know that working too much isn't your fault – it's not an unattractive or unsatisfactory feature. It's not simply because you're 'Type A' or have poor time-management skills. You are not the reason you feel like this. You are a product of our culture and conditioning, of the rules we are all taught and the effect these have on the body.

How did we get here?

Capitalism puts growth and profit above people, conditioning us to normalize chronic stress. In industrial nations, this has led to the least healthy generation ever, despite having access to resources that can support good health. Under this system, the worst outcomes are for women and groups that are marginalized.

The impact of living to work dysregulates our nervous system and keeps us stuck in a state of survival even when we are achieving our goals because our negativity bias *(see page 25)* is heightened, jacking up our fight-or-flight response and making it impossible to see the bigger picture. Our nervous system is the foundation for all that we are and all that we do, and the way we've been conditioned to work is dysregulating. Therefore, 'mindset,' 'how-tos,' and 'hacks' are short-lived and, frankly, create anxiety because, invariably, we use these short-term measures to suppress long-term terror.

Our conditioning normalizes chronic stress and anxiety and uses it as a productivity tool – we call it motivation. And this same conditioning creates a belief that this pattern will lead us to satisfaction. However, from infancy, our systems and institutions have conditioned us to view satisfaction with suspicion, often

YOU ARE NOT THE REASON YOU FEEL LIKE THIS. YOU ARE A PRODUCT OF OUR CULTURE AND CONDITIONING, OF THE RULES WE ARE ALL TAUGHT AND THE EFFECT THESE HAVE ON THE BODY.

mistaking it for complacency. Consequently, satisfaction feels like a hopeless endeavor, as it's always out of reach.

Satisfaction, a sign of emotional safety, feels abnormal, and anxiety is normalized. Anxiety is our body's way of telling us that we are under threat. It tells us there's a reason to be terrified. Pause here for a moment and let that sink in, then think about how casually we talk about feeling anxious in our day-to-day lives.

Our conditioning has made day-to-day feelings of terror in the pursuit of success we are scared to enjoy, normal. And our human need for rest, play, and space becomes something to be ashamed of.

We are not designed to live in constant states of terror. It ravages our life-force energy, and keeps us suspended in repetitive cycles and our bodies flooded with stress hormones such as cortisol and adrenaline. This leads to burnout, which the World Health Organization (WHO) recognizes as an 'occupational phenomenon' and describes as 'a syndrome conceptualized as resulting from chronic workplace stress that has not been successfully managed. It is characterized by three dimensions: feelings of energy depletion or exhaustion; increased mental distance from one's job, or feelings of negativism or cynicism related to one's job; and reduced professional efficacy.'[4]

Stress can also impact women and men differently due to several factors, including differences in hormones, brain chemistry, social roles, and coping mechanisms. Hormonal differences, such as fluctuations in estrogen and progesterone levels, can affect women's stress responses. According to researchers in the department of psychiatry and the Department of Neurology at Harvard Medical School, women's amygdalae, the part of the brain associated with stress and emotional processing, are significantly more responsive to negative stimuli than men's. Men have more activity in the prefrontal cortex, associated with rational decision-making.[5]

Racial injustice means that people of color are at a greater risk of the impacts of stress due to racial weathering. Racial weathering is a hypothesis by Dr. Arline Geronimus, who was a researcher in the Department of Public Health Policy and Administration at the University of Michigan in Ann Arbor. The weathering hypothesis states that chronic exposure to social and economic disadvantage leads to an accelerated decline in physical health outcomes and could partially explain racial disparities in a wide array of health conditions.

In a 2018 interview, Dr. Geronimus said, 'What I've seen over the years of my research and lifetime is that the stressors that impact people of color are chronic and repeated through their whole life course, and in fact may even be at their height in the young adult-through-middle-adult ages rather than in early life. And that increases a general health vulnerability – which is what weathering is.'[6]

BECOMING STRANGERS TO OURSELVES

Due to outdated gender roles, women often take on more caregiver roles and have greater responsibilities at home, which can lead to increased stress. As such, women may be less likely to engage in behavior that reduces stress, such as exercise and seeking support, because we are too busy meeting the needs of everyone else and desperately trying to succeed in our businesses or careers. Furthermore, we are bombarded with messages about having it all and tips to help us hack our minds and bodies – as if the remedy for doing too much is to find ways to do more! This leads to stress-increasing behavior, such as overthinking, and maladaptive coping strategies, such as 'doom scrolling' on social media, or using phrases such as 'wine o'clock' as excuses to indulge in drinking to relieve stress. Alternatively, we try to strategize our way out of it like it's a matter of discipline, will, and consistency. Burnout says, 'I can't cope,' and we try to squash it down with an action plan that includes self-care as a productivity tool. Under these conditions, caring for ourselves and meeting our needs become processes we use to return to former states of unsustainable levels of productivity.

Layers of productivity conditioning have made us become strangers to our essence, yet overly familiar with trying to succeed in a world that wasn't really built for us. The conditioning is so strong that we tell ourselves and each other micro-untruths (or big whoppers) that over time bury our needs, and we forget who we are.

But deep down, we know. This truth is nestled in our cells, joints, and soft tissue. It manifests as headaches when we try to do the thing we really want to but resist due to our fear of change. Or the anxiety we experience when our to-do list is bulging with too many tasks for the time we have allocated.

I became a stranger to my true essence because I believed that my lack of self-worth was my fault. It was my fault that I didn't fit into a narrow definition of success. When I looked around and compared myself to what society upheld as 'right,' it automatically made me 'wrong.' With this comparison in mind, I experienced myself as weak and incapable. I fell into the trap of believing that I was broken. This was easier to process than the existential conundrum of a rigged system designed to keep us in a hypnotic state of brokenness. I could control the idea that I was wrong. When everything feels out of control, we protect ourselves by internalizing issues so that we have a false sense of things being within our control. This is easier to manage than accepting that our system of governance is deeply ruptured.

Throughout school I learned that I was 'wrong' because my beauty is not pretty, according to the very narrow standard that is assigned to women. Academically, I was 'wrong' because I just didn't get the school system. As such, my potential was obvious, but my skill, consistency, and discipline were lacking.

When I entered the world of work, I understood that I had to work twice as hard because of conscious and unconscious biases and three times as hard because of my internalized biases of not being good enough. To prove myself as worthy, I became a people-pleaser, putting the feelings, needs, and perceptions of others before my own.

In my career as a coach, I see different versions of this story internalized by my clients and reflected back at me. Whether they struggled in school like I did or were gifted and talented 'good girls,' these women and I are bonded through using productivity and achievement to prove ourselves as being equal to white, able-bodied, heteronormative, middle-class men. We are taught that this is the path to self-worth and freedom.

How free do you feel when your life is built around working compulsively? Moving from one goal to the next in the hope that *one day* it will be enough for you to feel fulfilled? All while secretly believing that you have no option but to keep going because what would you do and who would you be without your work?

During a coaching session with a group of very successful female entrepreneurs, I asked them a question: 'How much does your success cost you?' The first response I got was, 'Too fucking much.' The other five women said things along the same lines:

- 'I can't afford to burn out but I can't afford to stop.'

- 'I'm anxious, lethargic, and irritable, but I'm terrified that if I slow down I'll lose everything and it would impact my family.'

- 'I don't know who I am outside work.'

- 'I'm making the type of money my ancestors couldn't dream of but emotionally and physically, I feel like I'm constantly overdrawn.'

I want to be clear: Your addiction to being productive is indeed an addiction. Although your productivity may feel like a conscious choice, this 'choice' is driven by layers of unconscious fears that were laid upon you under the guise of comfort like a snuggly blanket. Over time, even the snuggliest of blankets will feel cumbersome if you keep laying new on top of old. The trick is that these blankets are laid slowly from the day you're born so that you adjust to the weight, restriction, and temperature instead of learning when enough is enough. Until one day, if you're lucky, you realize that you're trapped with no room to look around, never mind grow and expand.

Embodiment Practice

Mindful Body Scan

For this exercise, you can sit, stand, or lie down. I suggest putting one hand on your heart and asking yourself if you want to sit, stand, or lie down for this practice and letting your body be your guide.

- Allow your eyes to gently scan your environment. When your eyes find where they want to rest, take a long, slow, deep breath in, slowly exhale, and if it feels good to do so, allow your eyes to close. If you do not want to close your eyes, soften your gaze.

- On your next exhalation, imagine any tension dissolving. This will help you to calm your mind and prepare for the body scan. On your next inhale, make sure your spine is straight and that you're comfortable.

- Begin the body scan, paying attention to the top of your head and noticing any sensations you may feel. You are just noticing the sensations, not labeling them. Then slowly move your attention downwards. Notice any sensations, feelings, or tensions you may have in each part of your body as you do this.

- As you scan your body, observe each sensation without judgment. Whether it's tension, relaxation, warmth, or coolness, simply notice it and allow it to be. This is a practice of observation and acceptance, not a time for criticism or analysis.

- If you notice any tension or discomfort in any area of your body, imagine sending your breath to that area. Picture your breath as healing energy, soothing and releasing the tension.

- Continue to move your attention down through your body, observing, accepting, and gently sending breath to areas of tension.

- Once you get to your feet, take a moment to feel your connection to the Earth. If you're lying down, imagine your feet being connected to the Earth. Imagine roots growing from the soles of your feet, grounding you and providing stability.

- When you're ready, pay attention to the surface of your skin, maybe wiggling your fingers and your toes to begin to bring this practice to an end.

- Return to your normal breath and slowly open your eyes: Take a moment to sit with the feelings of calm and groundedness before returning to your day.

This practice is one way to slow down, feel your feelings, be present with the contradictions of being human, and start treating your body with reverence and kindness. This practice can be done daily or whenever you feel the need to ground yourself and reconnect with your body.

//

GETTING TO KNOW THE SIGNS OF TOXIC PRODUCTIVITY

If you can begin to see some of the origins of why you work too much, it's a powerful first step. As inhumane levels of productivity are promoted as aspirational from a very young age, most people don't realize they are addicted to being productive. Here are some questions to help:

- Apart from sleep, are you able to rest without feeling guilty because you could be doing something 'constructive'?

- Do you fear running out of time or being 'too late' if you're not using your time efficiently?

- Are you constantly busy, with a to-do list of never-ending urgent tasks?

- Do you judge yourself by how you think others perceive you?

- Can you become over-controlling as a way of coping?

- Has anxiety become a motivational tool?

- Does everything you do trickle down to being more productive; for example, self-care for the sake of being more productive, or monetizing your hobbies?

- Do people tend to begin requests with statements such as, 'I know you're really busy but...'?

- When you're exhausted, do you default to thinking that it is because you lack organization or time-management skills?

- Do you take time off to relax for the sake of relaxing?

- Do you overlook your accomplishments?

- Does your self-care go out of the window when work is busy?

- Do you try to find ways of doing more in less time, even though you know this is impossible?

- When you go on holiday, are you able to be present or do you spend time:

  ~ Complaining about work?

  ~ Obsessing over your business?

  ~ Doing a bit of work to make things easier when you get back to work?

- If someone asks you about yourself, do you default to what you do for work?

- Do you put off meeting your own needs?

- Do you set impossibly high standards for yourself?

- Do you worry that if you allow yourself to fully feel you'll become overwhelmed by emotions like rage or grief?

- Deep down would you love to be seen completely for who you are, but simultaneously that terrifies you?

- Do you sense that something isn't 'right' but you fear the uncertainty of changing the status quo?

- Does all this make you feel like you're not being true to yourself and it's pissing you right off?

I'm going to ask you to hold three important ideas throughout this book. The first is to know and accept that if you answered yes to any, most, or all these questions, it's not your fault and it's not a sign that you need to 'fix' yourself because something in you is broken or that you need to work smarter and just be more efficient. The second is that you need to make peace with uncertainty. There is no short answer or quick fix. The answers we seek are in the feelings we have been taught to avoid. This brings me to the third idea: we need to understand that multiple things can be true at one time; therefore, we do not need to limit ourselves to toxic positivity. We can be sad and hopeful, angry and compassionate, clever and naive. When we can hold these seemingly contradictory states simultaneously, we allow ourselves the full spectrum of human experience without judgment, or self-censure. This paradoxical acceptance can lead to profound personal growth and a deeper, more-nuanced understanding of our own complexity and humanity beyond the binary of positive and negative. These aspects of our humanity do not denote weakness, but rather a richness of experience that contributes to our overall wholeness. In learning to hold these three ideas – acceptance of self without the need for 'fixing', making peace with uncertainty, and embracing the complexity of our emotional landscape – we begin the journey of authentic self-discovery and compassionate self-acceptance. You will also see that it is not you, it's the system.

We live in a society that conditions us from early childhood to value productivity above all else, to temper our emotions, to not be 'needy,' and to think rest is something to simply recharge our batteries so that we can get back to commodifying ourselves for profit we will not enjoy.

Changing the system starts with us being the change we want to see in our own lives. The first step is to own our discomfort with the status quo, to acknowledge that constantly striving for success but never feeling safe enough to fully relax or feel content is not living; this is existing. We must see that it doesn't help anyone if we're living on the edge of our nerves, ready to snap at any moment. We must understand that shutting down our feelings because we're terrified of what will surface is what will make us fall apart and that feeling our feelings is what will help us free ourselves and each other from the trap of toxic productivity.

When you start to feel how layer upon layer of conditioning has led you to a place of working too much, being everyone's caretaker, worrying about how you're perceived, hiding parts of yourself for fear of being 'too much' or not enough – just that understanding can be the start of something. A shift in perception. A momentary 'Aha, yes.' A seed of change sprouting roots and pushing through the soil.

It is in this start of something that change becomes hope. The next step is to pause, to see what emerges, to be curious and listen to the sounds we can hear beyond the rapid heart rate and shallow breath of survival. This pause will allow us to take some time to consider what is possible when we see, feel, and respect the intelligence of our biology, and how this can provide wisdom that will teach us how to thrive.

Joyful Practice

Savoring

This practice is one of my versions of Dr. Rick Hanson's 'Taking in the Good.'[7]

Taking in the Good is a mindfulness practice based on the idea that our brains have a 'negativity bias,' meaning they tend to focus on and remember negative experiences more than positive ones. This was a helpful survival mechanism for our ancestors but can lead to unnecessary stress and anxiety in our modern lives. With time and repetition, Taking in the Good can help us to pay more attention to things that enrich us and develop a positivity bias which will help us to have a greater appreciation of the everyday joys of life.

As you go through your day, make a point to notice the joyful moments. This could be a beautiful sunrise, a satisfying meal, a warm hug from a loved one, taking a break instead of powering through, or honoring your boundaries. Even the smallest good moments count – we don't leave joy on the table.

When you notice a joyful moment, take a few seconds to savor it. Allow yourself to fully feel the nourishment or satisfaction it brings. You might want to close your eyes to enhance your focus on the experience.

As you're savoring the experience, imagine the goodness sinking into you. Picture it as a warm light that's filling your body, or a Ready Brek glow surrounding you (if you know, you know). Imagine this good feeling becoming part of you.

Once the moment passes, take a few seconds to reflect and acknowledge that you've had an enriching experience and that's contributed to your well-being.

The more often you notice, savor, and absorb the good, the more natural it will become. Over time, you'll find that you begin to naturally notice joyful moments and savor them.

//

'All big things come from small beginnings. The seed of every habit is a single, tiny decision. But as that decision is repeated, a habit sprouts and grows stronger. Roots entrench themselves and branches grow. The task of breaking a bad habit is like uprooting a powerful oak within us. And the task of building a good habit is like cultivating a delicate flower one day at a time.'

James Clear, *Atomic Habits*

Dear One,

Your imperfections are perfectly designed
like streams that zigzag toward rivers that
wind their way toward the ocean.

At first glance, the stream looks small and
insignificant until you zoom out and see its evolution.

Your trickle kept you safe when you were taking
form, but now you must rise as an act of devotion.

CHAPTER 2

HOW YOU HAVE (MAL) ADAPTED

'The wounded child inside many females is a girl who was taught from early childhood that she must become something other than herself, deny her true feelings in order to attract and please others.'

bell hooks, *All About Love*

I hope that you're beginning to understand the origins of your addiction to work and productivity. I have no doubt that this stems from unsuspecting carers and educators during your formative years. And there's no blame here. Your carers and educators were working with the tools of their conditioning. Perhaps you were taught that work is the source of self-worth, a way to earn external validation with your productivity, to be 'good,' and to put the needs of others before your own. Maybe you learned that having desires of your own was selfish and that to be desirable you had to be a martyr. It's possible that you had to prove that you were not a burden or make up for not being 'good/pretty/cool/slim/clever enough.' Your story may have been hijacked by the story that had been projected onto you by the well-intended expectations of others – shout out to the Black and Brown parents' dreams of their children becoming doctors, barristers, and engineers!

Many of us have some understanding or know full well what's been going on, yet it seems impossible to disrupt this ingrained pattern. It feels like it's part of our DNA because it is hardwired through repetition over and over again. We've adapted to cope with the life circumstances and environments we frequent. Or, more accurately, we've maladapted, living in our survival physiology, which we're designed to inhabit in cases of emergency – hypervigilant, ready for anything, multi-tasking at home and work, people-pleasing, easily irritated, or one small step away from overwhelm. We might be fighting fires all day with just an ember left for our lives.

In this chapter, we're going to explore the deep-rooted connection between our bodies and minds, what's going on in our bodies when we live in a state of working too much and why our collective addiction to productivity is toxic to our very being.

RECONNECTING YOUR MIND AND BODY: EMBRACING INNER WHOLENESS

Your mind and body are one. Your brain is inside your body. I know this is obvious but most of us have been conditioned to function like it's not. Phrases such as 'mind over matter' and 'mindset work' are frequently heralded as a panacea for all ills. For a moment, I invite you to connect with your brain and acknowledge it as *part* of your biology rather than a tool for domination. Gently lay your hands on your hairline, then move them to your crown, followed by the back of your head and then the nape of your neck. As you lay your hands, see if you notice anything. Notice your reaction to the temperature of your hands – maybe touch makes your scalp feel more relaxed. You could feel something else or nothing at all. There is no wrong or right response; there is no objective – this is merely an invitation to form a relationship with your brain. This beautiful organ is like the operating system for your mind and deserves to be regarded as more than a tool that needs to be controlled with strategies and discipline.

The language we use repeatedly, and its origins, have created meanings suggesting that the mind and brain are separate but connected to the body. For centuries the body was considered as a vehicle for the brain, a lump of moving matter. In the 20th century, the concept of 'mind-body dualism' (Descartes)[1] was pervasive, suggesting that the mind and the body (matter) were separate in their nature.

Modern science recognizes that the mind and body are interconnected and that maintaining physical health is crucial for optimal brain function, mental health, and overall well-being. And vice versa. The understanding of the complex interactions between the brain, the body, and the environment has been evolving since the mid-20th century. In 1936, the Canadian physician Hans Selye proposed the concept of 'stress' and its effects on the body, which led to the development of the field of psychoneuroimmunology.[2] This is the study of how psychological factors affect the immune system and overall health. Research in this field and in psychosomatic medicine has highlighted the important role psychological and emotional factors can play in physical health and disease. Your body, including your brain, is an ecosystem of living organisms interacting with each other to form the complex system that is you.

Today, it is widely accepted that the body and brain are intimately connected. With my work, I invite you to go deeper and wider. To consider that not only are the body and mind one, but also that the mind, body, and our environment are one, making us all part of one whole. Like our planet, the body is a multidimensional, living, breathing, shape-shifting map. From arid deserts to oozing lava and water that births rivers, oceans, and streams, to logical bricks and mortar and bodily fluid that creates life in darkness, which is then birthed into light via the womb, our bodies are a reflection of the body that birthed us all: Earth.

NEEDS VERSUS SUCCESS

Our planet has needs. When the need for rain is not met, we get drought. Similarly, when our need for hydration is unmet, we become dehydrated. This we know for sure. Yet, when it comes to work, we often view our bodies and our needs as getting in the way of our success; for example, we ignore our need for hydration because we need to finish one sentence, which becomes a paragraph, which becomes the whole morning without taking a sip. Systemically, we ignore the Earth's need for rejuvenation and over-exploit her land for FTSE 100 profit. None of these are regenerative. In fact, they are *degenerative*, eroding our bodies and our planet, ravaging our collective life force, and depleting our energy reserves.

When we consider ourselves as whole, it's easier to appreciate the law of cause and effect, or Newton's third law: 'For every action, there is an equal and opposite reaction.' Internalizing this will create a greater appreciation for what is required to thrive rather than upholding the status quo that limits us to surviving. And this requires a response that respects the natural intelligence of our bodies, our planet, and understands our innate needs as a bid for care and connection. Tending to these bids as fundamental natural needs rather than inconveniences promotes a felt experience of safety and trust. This differs from our conditioning, which treats our nature (our body and our planet) as things to be dominated and controlled in exchange for productivity. We have reduced ourselves and our planet to resources that should be commodified. It's not by chance that the departments in workplaces that have responsibility for employees are called 'Human Resources.' Let's break this down further:

- **Human capital:** the term used to refer to the knowledge, skills, abilities, and other qualities individuals possess that enable them to perform a wide range of economic activities.

- **Resource:** a stock or supply of money, materials, staff, and other assets that can be drawn on by a person or organization to function effectively. This word likens humans to stock, a supply of money and materials.

- **Capital:** a valuable resource of a particular kind. In terms of human capital, a valuable resource based on what they do with no consideration for who they are and what they need.

Human skills, abilities, and other qualities are indeed important factors in economic growth and development. They are often cited as a precipitating factor in innovation. This is what supported our evolution as a species. Human capital (skills) can also play a critical role in promoting social mobility and reducing economic inequality by providing individuals with the skills and knowledge they need to succeed in the modern economy. But at what cost? And which individuals get to succeed in a system that discriminates against so many?

As a Black woman and person who thinks deeply, the terms 'human resources' and 'human capital' hold an even deeper meaning for me. It makes me think of times when people who look like me were considered to be nothing but a resource, capital that was brutally exploited for Western profit.

Our profit-driven mentality has all but relegated us from citizens into commodities and consumers, serving the interests of the super-rich – making our innate needs akin to a design flaw. This was further exacerbated by the Industrial Revolution, which was partly funded through the kidnap and commodification of enslaved Africans via the transatlantic slave trade.*

The Industrial Revolution had a profound impact on world culture. It led to the rise of urbanization, changes in social classes and family structures, the spread of mass media, and the emergence of consumer culture. It also spurred technological innovations that transformed art, literature, and music. Overall, the Industrial Revolution had a profound impact on the way people lived, worked, and thought about themselves and the world around them.

The Industrial Revolution reformed formal education, both in terms of content and access. The demand for skilled workers led to a greater emphasis on practical and standardized education as governments recognized a need for an educated workforce to meet the demand created by technological advancement. Schools began to teach subjects such as mathematics, science, and engineering to prepare students for the new job opportunities that were emerging. The role of a teacher went from religious education to subjects and skills that would support a workforce that was able to transition from manual labor, guided by natural cycles, to machine-based manufacturing in factories.

Prior to the Industrial Revolution, most workers were self-employed or worked alongside their families as farmers. With the growth of factories, workers began to sell their labor to factory owners in exchange for wages.

---

* As a Black woman who is directly impacted by the ways white supremacy has created a human hierarchy, I have first-hand experience of adapting to racism and those adaptations simultaneously becoming maladaptive. Therefore, it's important to note that my focus on the British Industrial Revolution in the early part of this chapter is not to center whiteness. It's to demonstrate the systemic and cultural impact the Industrial Revolution had on the way we've learned to work.

Technology created machines that could work at a faster rate than humans and produce more uniform products. Instead of these advancements making life easier, they led to longer working hours to meet the growing demand for consumer products. Many workers had to work 12- to 16-hour days, six days a week. A stark contrast to work organized around the seasons and natural rhythms of life. I'm not attempting to romanticize pre-industrial work, as it was laborious and generally took place from 'sunup to sundown.' In the Northern Hemisphere, farmers would work longer hours during planting and harvesting seasons but may have had more downtime during the winter. Countries and continents closer to the equator tended to take more breaks during the day due to the hot temperatures. The work was arduous but there was no expectation for people to do things consistently (the same, not changing) unless you were an enslaved African – in which case your life depended on it. Work was impacted by the environment whereas the Industrial Revolution expedited the process of work suppressing the environment as well as our humanity and our human needs.

WHAT ARE YOUR NEEDS AND WHY DO THEY MATTER?

Abraham Maslow was an American psychologist who wrote a paper entitled 'A Theory of Human Motivation' in 1943.[3] In this paper, he identified a hierarchy of needs humans need to fulfil in order to 'self-actualize,' also known as reaching your true potential. From a very young age, we are taught to aspire to self-actualization. I have a deep-rooted fear of not self-actualizing that will always be there; however, because I'm aware of it, I'm able to identify when I'm being motivated by my fear as this it makes me ignore my needs.

Maslow identified four needs that need to be met regularly for humans to be able to self-actualize.

The first need is physiological: This includes our need for air, water, food, shelter, sleep, clothing, and sex for reproduction.

I often remind my clients that we live in our physiology first, as they tend to believe that their limitations are purely due to mindset. Our most foundational needs are usually the first things we let go of when we are busy. I believe that this is in part because we call them 'basic' needs. Something we consider to be basic is easy to dismiss as unimportant.

In terms of our need for air, industrialization has made the quality of the air we breathe poor. According to the WHO, 99 percent of the global population breathes air that exceeds their guideline limits.[4] (I'd love to know who and where the 1 percent are!) As individuals, we tend to make our breathing shallow when we are stressed as our fight-or-flight response is activated (more on this in Chapter 3). Being busy all the time creates stress. When we are stressed and feel like we have endless deadlines, we skip meals or eat convenience food, so we don't get the nutrients we need to feel satiated and nourished. By the same token, we don't drink enough water, so we become dehydrated, which impacts our energy and brain function. We try to force our way out of this with caffeinated drinks, sugary foods, and adaptogens like Lion's Mane for a short-term energy boost. This leads us to become addicted to caffeine and dependent on supplements as a means of a fast and convenient 'high' to get us through. We don't get enough sleep because we are stressed, working long hours, and trying to squeeze life in around the edges. Lack of sleep has a significant impact on our health and, therefore, our overall functioning. But no amount of money, success, or adaptogenic supplements can make up for the impact a lack of sleep, inadequate nourishment, dehydration, and fatigue has on your body and your brain.

NO AMOUNT OF MONEY, SUCCESS, OR ADAPTOGENIC SUPPLEMENTS CAN MAKE UP FOR THE IMPACT A LACK OF SLEEP, INADEQUATE NOURISHMENT, DEHYDRATION, AND FATIGUE HAS ON YOUR BODY AND YOUR BRAIN.

The second need is safety: This includes personal security, adequate employment, resources, health, and property. When your body (which includes your mind) is overworked and you're not able to rest and replenish your energy, you tend to live in a state of constant alert or hypervigilance. This state is the antithesis of one of our most important needs: safety. When you don't feel safe in your body, no amount of money or accolades will make you feel safer. In fact, money and accolades become short-term distractions from the lack of safety you feel.

The third need is love and belonging: This includes friendship, intimacy, family, and a sense of connection. If we are in a state of survival and have learned that we earn our relationships by making ourselves convenient and useful to others, it will be very hard for us to have meaningful connections with them. The level of vulnerability necessary to have close, intimate relationships will feel overwhelming, which leads to holding back and saying what we think people want to hear instead of our truth. And this includes things such as not telling your partner that you like the way they wiggle their nose before they sneeze, not having boundaries with your clients, and not asking your boss to say your name correctly.

We cannot feel safe when we are withholding parts of ourselves to fit into relationships that are too restrictive. This is like living in a pair of trainers half a size too small. It might feel like a good idea on the shop floor, but in your life... ouch!

The fourth need is esteem: This includes respect, self-esteem, status, recognition, strength, and freedom. Our conditioning makes us live upside down: we often believe that respect, status, and recognition are needed before we can then give ourselves permission to meet our other needs. For example, thinking or saying things like: 'I'll get good sleep once I have launched my new product or been given a pay rise.' Through a toxic combination of conditioning and adapting, we often have a warped view of what will give us the respect, status, and recognition we desire. We can become addicted to external sources of esteem, when all along, if we were to tend to our foundational needs (physical, safety, and relationships), we would in turn nourish our self-esteem.

There is a fifth need: self-actualization. Unlike the other needs, self-actualization (reaching our true potential) is not needed for our survival. This need is about growth and flourishing. As we satisfy the foundational needs we refer to as 'basic,' they become less urgent and our desire to self-actualize gains strength. Working towards self-actualization evokes a profound sense of fulfilment, satisfaction, and pride.

However, a culture that devalues our fundamental needs by normalizing toxic levels of productivity makes self-actualization feel unsafe. Self-actualization does not require endless striving. Self-actualization requires you to trust that your worth is inherent, to have healthy boundaries, and maintain healthy habits. This rhythm of 'being' rather than (over-) doing will feel unsatisfying and even perilous in a system that glorifies the immediate gratification gained from constant hard work and the perpetual striving it entails.

This pursuit and striving come from a place of lack. When our foundational needs are continuously unmet, we activate our survival physiology.

> *'When we are tired, we are attacked by*
> *ideas we conquered long ago.'*
> **Friedrich Nietzsche**

As we aim for self-actualization, our malnourished foundational needs churn and rumble, amplifying feelings of scarcity and deficiency. No amount of success can ever compensate for chronic exhaustion, for persistently going over our bandwidth. No status, accolades, or influence can rectify the imbalance created when women shoulder the majority of emotional, domestic, and caregiving responsibilities, whether at home, work, or within interpersonal relationships. No pay rises will compensate for the police frequently stopping you in your luxury car because of the color of your skin.

Under these circumstances, self-actualization goes from being a fulfilling adventure of growth and abundance to a hazardous escape from deficit and struggle. Because underneath the veneer of success is self-doubt and struggle. Under these conditions, self-worth is hinged on your latest success and your ability to devote your energy to profit-making activity. As such, self-actualization becomes a function to prove yourself as worthy of acceptance.

Reconnect and Listen

A Self-Care Exercise to Nurture Your Needs

Our culture of individualism can make us hyper-individual, and this state of self-reliance and self-focus makes it difficult to trust our needs because they are seen as obstacles. This often makes our human need for support feel as if we're being 'too needy.' In this exercise, I'm inviting you to receive support and ask your body what you need.

You will need a wall or a sofa and a floor. You may need a blanket if it's cold.

- Lie down on your back with your legs up against a wall. If you do not have enough wall space for that, lie on the floor with your legs on a sofa so that your calf muscles are resting on the seat of the sofa. Wriggle your body so that your bottom is as close to the wall or sofa as you can manage.

- If you have tight hamstrings or knee problems, it might be more comfortable to choose the sofa option.

- Feel your connection to the ground beneath you and the wall or sofa. On your next exhale, allow yourself to let go so that you feel heavier on the ground. If it feels good, allow your eyes to gently close. If this does not feel good, soften your gaze.

- Connect with your breath – no need to alter it; this is an invitation to become aware of your breath. Observe your breath and let it tell you what you need.

- On your next exhalation, invite your body to soften even more. Notice how it feels to allow the ground to support you. If you can, imagine the Earth holding you gently.

- Take a few breaths here and notice how it feels to allow yourself to be held.

- On your next exhalation, allow your shoulders to rest heavier on the floor. And then, on your next inhalation, imagine breathing into your pelvis. As you exhale, let go of any tension.

- Put one hand on your heart and one on your stomach. Witness the rise and fall of each breath. Pay attention to your hand on your heart and ask yourself what you need. There is no need to do anything. This is an opportunity for you to listen to your needs. Meet yourself with compassion. You may identify one need or several; you may not identify anything, or you could feel numb. The only objective here is to connect with your body, ask yourself what you need, and witness yourself without judging yourself or squashing your feelings down.

- Stay here as long as it feels good.

Reflection Questions

1. How did it feel to have your legs up against the wall or on the sofa – were there any sensations of relief, discomfort, or a neutral feeling?

2. How did it feel to let go and be held by the ground?

3. What did you notice when you asked yourself about your needs?

4. How did it feel to be a witness to your needs?

///

HOW OUR NERVOUS SYSTEM ADAPTS WHEN WE SIDELINE OUR NEEDS

I am not a nervous system expert. I have completed various training courses in relation to the nervous system and human behaviors. I have been able to distil my learning into language that is relatable, to create practical examples and share practices that help people get to know their nervous system. I have shared my knowledge in workshops, coaching groups, and keynote presentations. The feedback has always included people telling me they understand themselves differently or they feel relieved because they realize they are not 'broken.'

What Is the Nervous System and Why Is It Important?

I describe our nervous system as the foundation of who we are and how we are.

We have many nervous systems. The focus of my work, however, is the autonomic nervous system, as this is the nervous system that governs our survival and our social engagement. For context, I'm going to touch on three nervous systems and then focus on the autonomic nervous system and how it relates to the way we have learned to work.

1. **The central nervous system (CNS), which is the brain and spinal cord.**

To make this real, and help you form a connection with your CNS, I invite you to take the palm of your hand and lay it on your forehead, then move it up to your hairline, then your crown, the back of your head, then the nape of your neck. This is where your brain meets your brain stem. The brain stem connects your brain to your spinal cord. Now place both your hands so you can feel where the nape of your neck meets your back, and as best you can, lay your palms down all the way down your spine until you touch your tailbone. It's at the very bottom of your spine between your buttocks and just above your anus.

You have just connected with your CNS and tracked the network of nerves that come together to help determine how we perceive, respond to, and interact with the world around us.

Our bodies are a highly sophisticated sensory system. Our senses (sensors) send data to our CNS, and it translates the information to create our perception of the world around us. It regulates and coordinates voluntary movements, such as when we decide to clap our hands, as well as reflexes such as flinching when we hear the buzzing of a bee. Reflexes happen below the level of consciousness. We do not need to think to react, we just do, which is why we often flinch at the buzzing bee before we see it.

The CNS is responsible for maintaining internal homeostasis (harmony), including regulating unconscious functions such as your heart rate, breathing, and digestion. Generally, you do not have to think in order for your heart to function, to breathe, or to digest food. Your body is constantly working for you.

It also processes information based on your experience and stores it in your memory for later use, which can be helpful or unhelpful. Your CNS is also involved in regulating your emotions, motivation, and decision-making processes.

2. **The peripheral nervous system (PNS), which encompasses the nerves the flow outward from the CNS.**

I'm going to talk about the somatic nervous system and autonomic nervous system separately because of the way they relate to how many of us experience work. The PNS goes from your head to your feet and everything in between. I have a guided meditation called 'Your Perfect Palms,' where I invite you to lay the palms of your hands all over your body. Doing this helps you connect with your body as a whole. It is a compassionate way to explore how it feels to be you and will give you a sense of the landscape of your PNS. You can listen to it on my website (see page 259) or in the audiobook.

For now, I invite you to lay a hand on your temple and gently run your hand down one side of your body, then take your other hand and run it down the other side – don't forget to include your feet. Then gently run your hand down the length of your arm to your fingertips and do the same on the other side. Now place your hands flat on your stomach so they are touching at your belly button and gently move them outward towards your sides. If you can, place your palms flat on your back so they meet at your spine, then gently move them toward your side. You have just mapped your PNS.

Together, your CNS and PNS coordinate and control your body's movements, sensations, thought processes, and other vital functions – how cool is that?! There is no tech that can match the refinement and elegance of your nervous system.

3. **The autonomic nervous system (ANS), which regulates involuntary bodily functions.**

The autonomic nervous system (ANS) is a division of the peripheral nervous system that controls the automatic (autonomic), unconscious functions of your body, including regulating your heart rate, digestion, respiration, and other internal functions that are not consciously directed. If we had to consciously direct all our bodily functions, we would feel bombarded and overloaded. As I'm typing this, I'm looking at the screen and my fingers know where to go without me thinking about it. I'm breathing and can hear cars on the road outside. I'm also noticing that I'm thirsty and realize that I have been slightly holding my breath as I'm excited to share this information with you. If I had to consciously think about all the things I'm doing simultaneously, I would be overwhelmed.

To connect with your ANS, I invite you to put your right hand on the back of your neck and your left hand on your heart. Take a few deep breaths here. Leave your left hand on your heart and place your right hand on the lower part of your stomach. Although it does not have a defined endpoint, this is an area of your body that is controlled by the ANS.

Before I go into more detail about the two branches of the ANS, I want you to reflect on the practice of connecting with your nervous system and think about what you noticed. For example, when I have one hand on the back of my neck and the other on my heart, I nearly always feel energy moving down the left side of my neck to my heart. The first time I put my hands on my heart and my stomach, I felt intense sorrow. I'm not saying that you should feel anything; I offer this as a compassionate somatic enquiry for you to connect with how *you* feel.

The ANS has two branches: the sympathetic nervous system and the parasympathetic nervous system.

The sympathetic nervous system prepares the body for action, often referred to as the 'fight-or-flight' response (and which also includes the 'freeze' and 'fawn' responses), by increasing heart rate, dilating pupils, and releasing adrenaline and other hormones. 'Freeze' is when there is a lot of sympathetic activity inside, but the outside appears to be disconnected and shut down. And 'fawn,' a term coined by the therapist Pete Walker,[5] describes a state where the tendency is to people-please, appease, and pacify the threat.

The parasympathetic nervous system, on the other hand, counterbalances the sympathetic nervous system by slowing heart rate, contracting pupils, and promoting rest and digestion. The two branches of the ANS work together to maintain balance in the body and to respond to internal and external stimuli.

Nervous system dysregulation occurs when the nervous system is in a state of continual or repeated activation or in extended conditions of stress. Simply put, we spend too much time with the sympathetic nervous system switched on, in that fight, flight, freeze, or fawn mode, and not enough time in 'rest-and-digest' mode, which is the role of the parasympathetic nervous system. We rarely come back to a balanced state of homeostasis as our foot is constantly on the accelerator.

Physical effects can include memory problems, insomnia, dizziness, fatigue, and digestive problems. And the potential psychological effects include fear of being seen, anxiety, people-pleasing, hyper-vigilance, overworking, lack-based thinking, planning for the worst, feeling unsafe in your body, feeling isolated, easily overwhelmed, needing to control/win/be good/right, and being addicted to negative reinforcement.

HIGH-FUNCTIONING FREEZE

Women who work too much are often trapped in a state of what I refer to as 'high-functioning' freeze. This is when there is a lot of activity taking place on top of a frozen layer, unconsciously trapping feelings and emotions that haven't been processed, and therefore feel overwhelming.

For many of us, our conditioning has been for toxic productivity and toxic productivity only. From the moment we were eggs in the embryonic wombs of our mothers, who were foetuses in the wombs of our grandmothers, we were primed for productivity. In our world, where everything and everyone is valued according to the speed and capacity at which they become a profitable commodity, emotions and feelings are deemed to be obstacles that get in the way. As such, we are programmed to subdue our feelings with 'mindset' and disassociate from our felt sense with 'strategy.'

When we become accustomed to disassociating from events we can't handle, it becomes the default setting for the way we do life, full stop. These patterns usually begin in childhood, when we learn to adapt who we are in exchange for acceptance by holding emotions and suppressing parts of ourselves so that we are not rejected.

It becomes maladaptive when you're an adult with a desire to grow into your fullness. Growth tends to awaken parts you usually freeze for protection. As these feelings and emotions start to arise, it can feel terrifying, leading you to do what has become instinctual – to freeze. And so, the cycle repeats.

We try to over-function our way out.

But we can't.

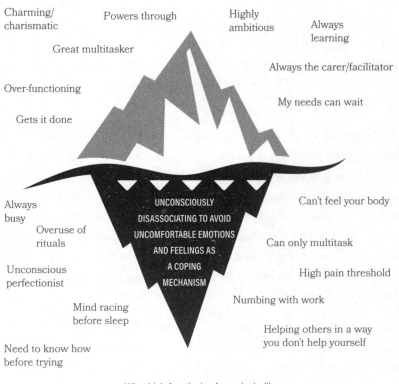

What high-functioning freeze looks like

THE THAW

At the beginning of 2020, the world succumbed to mass chaos and uncertainty prompted by a pandemic that decimated populations and broadcast uncomfortable global truths that could no longer remain suppressed. The deliberate marginalization of people who do not neatly tuck into white supremacist, patriarchal, ableist, heteronormative, neurotypical, toxic capitalist ideals and the way that intersects with the hierarchy of race was displayed on TV screens from Freetown, Sierra Leone to London, England.

For many, the icy layer that protected them from the truths that had been frozen in their nervous systems was forced to thaw by heated global events. From forests ablaze due to environmental damage to protesters gaslighted by authorities whose empathy did not extend to communities that are marginalized, women, and environmental issues.

The enforced stillness of lockdown compelled people to look inwards. This interoception (signals that you sense from within your body) brought many people face to face with estranged truths that were beginning to emerge through an activated nervous system. Activity that indicated that managing overwhelm by keeping abandoned emotions immobile and suspended in an icy nervous system was no longer an option.

You don't need any more strategies or plans. You need to learn how to work with yourself and nurture your growth instead of turning yourself into a project to manage.

When we make the conscious decision to make changes to support the growth we want, it is essential for us to do the work necessary for our nervous system to feel safe enough to facilitate these changes.

This requires more than a new mindset. To recover from this way of being, we must work with the natural intelligence of the body.

That's where our journey takes us next.

Joy Practice

Get Your Groove on, aka Dance!

This activity is designed to induce joy. It is informed by positive psychology, neurobiology, and playful childhood nostalgia!

For those of you who think that dancing is a frivolous pursuit or confined to nights out, here is some data for you:

- Research on mood after various brief exercise and sports modes by Jingu Kim and Sungwoon Kim at the University of Florida suggested that dancing to hip-hop boosted well-being, reduced psychological distress and fatigue, elevated energy and mood, and lowered levels of stress.[6]

- An article in the *Greater Good Magazine* by UC Berkeley entitled 'Four Ways Dancing Makes You Happier'[7] cites various research about the impact of dancing on mental health and emotional well-being, including lowering the stress hormone cortisol, and increasing confidence, decreasing depression, and strengthening cultural connections.

- This simple-yet-effective activity engages your body's relaxation response. Dancing is a physical activity that can activate a sense of freedom, joy, and connection; all qualities that promote being in a ventral state (more on that in the next chapter). Listening to music from your youth helps to invoke childhood nostalgia, reminding you of more carefree times.

You don't have to dance to hip-hop, but the task is to dance. Cast your mind back to middle school and think about a pop song that makes you smile and reminisce on fun times at school or elsewhere. Perhaps a memory of an end-of-year disco or a song that inspired you or made you feel powerful. Play that song and dance.

Don't worry about how you dance – just move your body, remember, and enjoy.

At the end of the track, slow down, close your eyes, and pay attention to how your body feels. Is your body warmer? Do you feel more alive? Are you feeling joy?

This takes less than five minutes.

For some community joy, ask your friends to share songs that make them reminisce and recall good times. I did this with my friends – we were instantly filled with joy and making playlists!

///

Dear One,

You defied the greatest odds to be here,
exactly as you are, in this moment.

Out of 400 trillion options your biology
and the Divine chose you.

The number of ancestors that came together
for your creation is unfathomable.

You are a miracle.

Every tissue. Every cell. Every roll. Every
wrinkle is a technological marvel to behold.

When you become your own best friend,
your life will begin to unfold.

CHAPTER 3

BE YOUR NERVOUS SYSTEM'S BEST FRIEND

*'The real problem of humanity is the following:
We have Paleolithic emotions; medieval
institutions; and god-like technology. And
it is terrifically dangerous, and it is now
approaching a point of crisis overall.'*

Edward O. Wilson

When I turned 38, I felt like my life was bursting at the seams. I had spent so long holding myself in and living at my edges, I didn't realize I was grasping at threads. I was frayed and worn; no amount of patching up with mindset or hard work would mend the damage. I realized I was delicate like silk but had been treating myself like Teflon. All the energy my youth had generously loaned me now sent an overdue bill that my body refused to settle. My body had had enough and let me know with endless sinus and throat issues, heart palpitations, anxiety, and lethargy.

Forty was on the horizon and I was filled with dread – not due to my advancing age but due to the terror of nearing the peak of womanhood yet experiencing nothing like what I had read in magazines as a teenager. According to the headlines that formed some of my subconscious programming, life was about to begin. I was about to enter the prime of my life where I should be gloriously successful, financially free, and enjoying a vibrant sex life on a par with that of a 21-year-old man. In short, I should have been high on the crest of my best life. Meanwhile, I was experiencing what felt like my lowest ebb.

My GP was convinced that I was experiencing severe-moderate depression, and a psychological assessment informed me that I was experiencing anxiety and panic attacks. But deep within me, it felt more primal, fundamental, and ethereal. It was as if spirit wanted to reclaim its home – my body – while my brain viewed it as a hostile takeover. I felt raw and sensitive. I kept feeling like if one more thing was added to my plate I would topple over. I looked into the eyes of my beautiful child and worried about what I was role-modeling. I wanted to enjoy being a parent. I wanted my daughter to enjoy me being her mum. I was filled with guilt about constantly scraping up energy for parenting because work and worry consumed it all. Something had to give, and there was no way I was going to let that thing be how I showed up for my child.

I sought solace in self-help books and in well-being podcasts, but they often left me feeling chastised rather than comforted. The mantras about manifesting my reality and the world being a projection of my perspective felt like gaslighting and bullshit. I didn't manifest the racism I experienced, unless you say my skin manifested it because it's a beautiful, deep, earthy, rich shade of brown. I didn't choose to be a woman; it was a gift assigned at conception; I didn't manifest patriarchal standards that undermine my womanhood and say that I'm less than a man. My toxic productivity addiction was not by choice; it was by design, a reaction to a system constructed for me to believe that my ability to exploit myself was a measure of my worth. I didn't manifest low self-esteem: it was a by-product of a system that sought to diminish the miraculous potential of my body into a mere reproductive tool generating life, energy, love, and care in exchange for direct and indirect profit.

BEFRIENDING VULNERABILITY

After much futile searching, I came across the world of positive psychology, and it felt like a homecoming to the science of human flourishing. It wasn't about armoring myself with toxic positivity or making myself convenient. It was an invitation to journey inwards and to connect with a deep, inner knowing that there was more to life than what I was experiencing.

Positive psychology is a branch of psychology that began in 1998. It focuses on the study of positive experiences that contribute to human flourishing. It could be said that traditional psychology focuses on mental and emotional ill health, and positive psychology focuses on mental and emotional well-being. It focuses on building and expanding positive human experience, such as happiness, optimism, resilience, personal strengths, and fulfilling relationships. The aim of positive psychology is to support human thriving at an individual, community, and systemic level by sharing scientifically tested strategies to support positive feelings, behaviors, and thoughts without bypassing the complexity of life.

Positive psychology led me to the work of Brené Brown and her Ted Talk on the power of vulnerability.[1] Her roots in social work and her nuanced, intersectional lens were a breath of fresh air. Obviously, I stalked her work, and came across the famous quote in her book *The Gifts of Imperfection*: 'We cannot selectively numb emotions, when we numb the painful emotions, we also numb the positive emotions.'[2] It was a confronting truth, an awakening. I realized that in my dance to sidestep discomfort, I was inadvertently silencing my capacity to truly feel. By avoiding fear and pain, I was inadvertently avoiding life itself.

This led me to the field of somatics* and the transformative impact of working in partnership with your body rather than suppressing it. I decided I wanted to study somatic coaching so that I could

---

* Somatics is a field of study and practice that focuses on the connection between the mind and body, and includes things like mindfulness, movement, and posture, healing, and self-care.

integrate it into my coaching practice. On reflection, I think this was a soul calling that my body sneaked past my brain under the guise that it would help me with my work. As destiny (or internet tracking) would have it, I opened Facebook and there was an advert for Somatic Coach Training with The Somatic School.

The word 'Soma' is the ancient Greek word for the vibrant living body. Traditional coaching has a heavy focus on intellectualizing issues to reach a quick solution. We often refer to this as 'mindset.' But the mind is only part of the equation – as such, talking provides limited sustainable change.

At its core, somatic coaching understands the body as a sophisticated ecosystem that includes the mind. The mind permeates every cell in the body.[3] This approach acknowledges the latest research revealing humans as integrated neuro-psycho-biological beings. Our neurology, psychology, and biology are woven together like fabric. They can't be separated; this encapsulates the word soma – the whole body in its full aliveness.

During my training, I discovered the profound impact our biology, particularly our nervous system, has on our psychology. Learning about the dynamic interplay between our body and mental state reinforced the importance of incorporating a holistic approach to well-being and personal growth.

As I engaged in more somatic education, I began to feel like I belonged to myself. I felt grounded and connected for the first time, no numbing or distraction – just me, myself, and I (the De La Soul version, of course). I became aware that my automatic response to challenges and difficult emotions was to detach from my body. As I began to fully inhabit myself, I was struck by an intense surge of rage within. Rage that sneaked up before I had the chance to rationalize it and make it palatable – girls like me learned very quickly that we could not be seen to be angry because it would be seen as aggressive, a characteristic that could prevent me from achieving success and external validation. This rage didn't care for respectability politics and performance. Me being grounded and cultivating more emotional safety meant that feelings that had been frozen began to thaw and make themselves known. The main theme of my rage was fury about the ways in which my conditioning had deprived me of my full human experience.

When I allowed myself to befriend this rage, I was amazed to find hope and joy. Brené was right! Knowing that my rage did not obliterate my hope or my joy was liberating and transformative. I didn't have to be positive all the time to have a positive experience. I could acknowledge my feelings and tend to them instead of fearing that I would be engulfed. It was like being given the manual I should have had all along. It resonated with the eloquent description of joy in Theopedia: 'Joy is a state of mind and an orientation of the heart. It is a settled state of contentment, confidence, and hope.'[4]

My life became clearly demarcated by my training with The Somatic School and its founder, Nathan Blair. There was life before The Somatic School and then life enriched with embodied wisdom afterwards. I have done and will continue to do further training in relation to the power of our biology. The growth and experiences I've had since embarking on this path have affirmed and broadened my appreciation of life in its raw, authentic form. My idea of success has shifted from goals that look good on paper to a life that feels grounded, nourishing, and whole. My true purpose has been reconfirmed: to be part of a movement to help liberate women from the tyranny of toxic productivity by cultivating a culture of meaningful connection and belonging – to ourselves, at home, at work, in relationships, and to our planet.

Self-Reflection Journal Prompts

- Reflect on your adolescent years. What narratives or ideas were prevalent about reaching the age of 40 (or any significant 'milestone' age)? How might these perceptions have influenced your beliefs and expectations about this age?

- Can you think of instances when you felt the need to ignore your feelings because of how others might see (judge) you or because of your past experiences? How do you think this might have impacted your physical health or emotional well-being?

- Recall a moment when you felt a deep connection with your body, where you understood and tended to your needs effectively. What was happening around you or what were you doing that helped this feeling of connection?

- How would you describe the experience of being entirely in tune with your body, fully understanding your needs and how to fulfill them? What helps create this level of connection?

- Imagine considering your body as a sacred space interconnected with the universe. How would this impact the way you treat yourself?

- Reflect on your childhood and adolescence. What did you learn about adulthood? How might this have shaped your experience of adulthood?

- Pause for a moment and tune into your body. How does it feel to reflect on these questions? Are there any specific feelings or emotions emerging for you at this moment?

Grounding Practice

Whether these questions brought up tricky emotions or not, let's take a moment to ground into the present.

- Allow your eyes to wander around your environment. When you find something that attracts your attention, take a deep, slow breath in through your nose, then exhale gently through your mouth. If it feels good to do so, allow your eyes to gently close. Repeat the deep breaths three more times. Allow yourself to become fully present in this moment by bringing your attention to where your body is connecting to whatever you're sitting, standing, or lying on. As you do this, imagine your energy returning to your body and filling you up, so you feel heavy, anchored, grounded.

- Reflect on the journal prompts. What came up for you? What sensations did you experience? How did this make you feel?

- If you're feeling discomfort, notice and name the feelings, as this will help to soften them and help you take ownership of the feelings instead of them owning you. For example, *my chest feels heavy, like sadness.* Remember, your feelings are normal and part of the human experience. It's OK to feel them.

- See if you can breathe into your feelings by imagining your breath flowing into the areas of your body where you feel the emotions strongly. And then imagine parts of those feelings disappearing like mist when you exhale.

- Offer yourself some reassurance by speaking to these feelings gently, as if you're comforting a friend. You might say, 'It's OK to feel sad at this moment. I'm here, and I'm listening.'

- Use the power of your imagination to visualize a tranquil place where you feel calm, safe, and relaxed. It could be a place you've been to, or a place you've imagined. Try to involve all your senses. What can you see, hear, smell, touch, or taste in this imaginary place?

- Note how your body feels in this place of safety and think about where else you feel this sense of peace in your life.

- We are going to bring this practice to a close. When you feel ready, bring your awareness back to the present moment and know that this sense of peace is within you. Gently wiggle your fingers and toes, take a deep breath, and slowly open your eyes.

- Take a moment to journal about whatever came up for you.

You can access the audio version of this practice on my website *(see page 259)* and in the audiobook.

//

EMBODIED RESPONSES TO SYSTEMIC PRESSURES

Our bodies serve as intricate sensory systems, finely attuned to detect signals of safety or danger in the world (neuroception), shaping our psychology in ways often beyond our conscious awareness.

Under the oppressive trinity of capitalism, patriarchy, and white supremacy, our bodies are in a constant state of heightened vigilance, sensing the looming presence of danger. Those who face systemic marginalization experience an even greater onslaught of these danger signals. Women and people socialized as girls have been conditioned to believe that by pleasing others, not having needs, being convenient, and sacrificing ourselves (fawning), we can overcome this danger with success.

Yet, when we inevitably fall short of the impossible standards imposed upon us, we are led to believe that we are somehow lacking, whether in ambition or skills, and the solution lies in better time management, organization, or self-improvement. But no amount of mindset work, self-care retreats, beautifully designed planners, or even age-defying creams can create a sense of safety within a culture rooted in the oppressive trinity. Our bodies live our truth, no matter how hard we try to ignore it.

'The brain is an end-organ and is impacted by the nervous system and the body. This is why techniques that solely focus on 'retraining the brain' often miss the boat at restoring FULL nervous system regulation.'

Irene Lyon

In my work, my focus is on the autonomic nervous system (ANS), which I introduced in the previous chapter. It is the part of the nervous system that is responsible for regulating many of your body's automatic functions like heartbeat, digestion, and breathing; and is divided into two main branches: the sympathetic nervous system (SNS) prepares the body for action, while the parasympathetic system (PNS) is responsible for the 'rest-and-digest' response. The parasympathetic and sympathetic branches of the ANS provide opposing functions to maintain the body's homeostasis (balance); for example, inhale (ANS) and exhale (PNS).

When the SNS is activated, it prepares our bodies to go, from waking up and getting out of bed, to strenuous activity such as exercise, preparing for a presentation, or responding to a threatening situation. It increases our heart rate, blood pressure, and adrenaline levels, priming us for action.

Short SNS Exercise

- If you're sitting down, stand up.

- If you're standing, jump up and down.

- If you're unable to stand, lift and lower your arms.

///

Your SNS helped you to do that. And it is highly likely that you inhaled as you took action. In normal conditions that inhale activates the SNS and primes you to take action. The SNS often gets a bad rap because we associate it with survival, but it has many other vital functions. I hope you reflect on this every once in a while and remember how incredible your body is!

The parasympathetic system, on the other hand, conserves energy by slowing the heart rate and creating the conditions necessary for us to eat and digest food so that we benefit from the nutrients. It supports slowing down, restoration, and connection.

When our lives are in balance, there is a healthy interchange of activation (sympathetic) and relaxation (parasympathetic) throughout the day. The problem arises when our bodies are trapped in a perpetual state of stress or activation, throwing this delicate balance off-kilter. The lifestyle we live where we are constantly busy, juggling tasks and hurtling toward deadlines creates chronic levels of stress. Our culture of toxic productivity normalizes this pattern and calls it motivation, willpower, a strong work ethic, or being disciplined. This incessant pressure keeps our bodies in a state of hyper-arousal; we are hypervigilant, primed for high alert, triggering the sympathetic system non-stop and, because we are so adaptable, fight, flight, or freeze becomes normalized. Physical symptoms of hyperarousal include headaches, difficulty sleeping, and feeling restless.

Being on high alert around the clock ravages our life-force energy. It drains our precious resources, leaving us at risk of plummeting into the depths of our parasympathetic system. This is known as the dorsal state or 'hypo-arousal,' where the body 'shuts down' as a means of protection because the situation is perceived as inescapably threatening. We might feel apathetic in this state, or suffer from symptoms of chronic fatigue and auto-immune disorders.

And because we are not taught how to nourish ourselves, we tend to use the force of our fight-or-flight system to 'yank' ourselves out of shut-down, creating a boom-and-bust cycle that is unsustainable.

When these states become habitual, they become traits, and we believe they are a part of who we are. We start to believe we are an 'anxious' person, or prone to emotional outbursts, a born pessimist, or someone who is fearful or risk-averse. The intensity of living between the constant fluctuations of a 'boom-or-bust' lifestyle can make 'being in balance' – the state of homeostasis, where our sympathetic and parasympathetic systems are in harmony – feel unfamiliar. Instead, we're constantly primed for action, and we've been so conditioned to view rest and play as 'laziness,' a sign of being unproductive or unsuccessful, that our natural need for recuperation feels shameful and is therefore suppressed.

This continuous work-and-no-play mode, perpetuated by societal expectations and pressures, is meant to go on until retirement. Only then are we 'allowed' to rest and enjoy the fruits of our labor. But this model is flawed and harmful, taking a toll on our bodies, our minds, our overall well-being, and how we relate to ourselves and each other. Being productive, resting, and playing can coexist harmoniously. When this happens, we feel safe, and this allows our autonomic nervous system to function optimally and healthily.

LIBERATION BEGINS IN THE BODY

The journey to freedom and balance begins with cultivating self-awareness. By exploring our survival patterns, we can identify the needs beneath the state, needs that might otherwise remain hidden beneath a flurry of automatic reactions. Such introspection may not always be comfortable, but it is a critical step towards healing and growth.

Our survival responses – freeze, fawn, fight, and flight – represent the body's natural protective mechanisms, evolved over millennia to help us navigate the perils of a dangerous world. In the face of perceived threats, these responses activate, intending to keep us safe. They are not aberrations or a sign of personal failure. They are our biology doing exactly what it's designed to do.

However, the relentless stress and demands of our modern society often keep these survival states activated when they are designed to help us navigate finite periods of acute stress. The realities of structural inequality, systemic racism, patriarchal norms, and the relentless pace of capitalist productivity can feel, to our biological systems, like a constant state of threat.

> 'When our SEEKING system is pulled into the service
> of only pursuing tasks, goals, solutions, and success, its
> primary purpose of maintaining connection is subverted to
> the point it eventually gives up and we fall into despair.'
> **Bonnie Badenoch, The Heart of Trauma**

Despite all the cultural and technological advances we have experienced, our bodies, nervous systems, and brains have hardly evolved past our ancient ancestors, the hunter-gatherers. They lived in a world where a rustle in the bushes could be the difference between being the predator or the prey. We are biologically wired for that environment, finely attuned to react to life-or-death situations. Although we live in an unrecognizably different world, our bodies have not evolved past reacting as if those primitive threats still linger. Meeting deadlines, striving to be a 'good mother,' making ourselves conveniently available to others, avoiding setting boundaries for fear of being seen as difficult – these can all be perceived as threats to our survival.

In this modern era, change is still often perceived as a threat by our bodies. Your body does not differentiate between real and imagined danger. Any risk, even the risk associated with positive change, can send your nervous system into survival mode. We're wired to prioritize survival over growth. This is an inherent protective mechanism that was incredibly useful for our hunter-gatherer ancestors. Yet in our present world, this survival instinct can often become a barrier to our growth and development. We even have colloquial sayings such as, 'better the devil you know.' It is sentiments like this that enable oppressive systems to continue. My coaching practice is full of women who recognize that they require support to unlearn the conditions that make them feel unsafe so they can create new conditions that enable them to tolerate the discomfort and uncertainty that come with their desire for growth and transformation.

The fear of the unknown that comes with growth can also be experienced as a threat. Our tendency to be risk-averse is not self-sabotage, a limiting belief, or due to us not wanting success badly enough. It's our body's way of trying to protect us from potential harm. To thrive in our modern world and dismantle the oppressive trinity of capitalism, white supremacy, and patriarchy, we need to cultivate inner safety and conscious awareness. We must become aware of risks, not avoid them, so that we can differentiate real threats from perceived ones. This will also enable us to take action that is aligned with our greater good, rather than intense reactions that lack longevity. An example of this is the Black Lives Matter uprising in 2020, which was followed by corporates pledging their commitment to equity. In the months following the murder of George Floyd in May 2020, Diversity, Equity, and Inclusion (DE&I) roles rose by 55 percent according to the Society for Human Resource Management in the USA.[5] However, three years later these roles have been cut by 33 percent.[6] In 2022, the UK former Secretary of State for Health and Social Care Sajid Javid demanded urgent action to cut DE&I roles in the NHS as part of his 'war against waste and wokery.'[7]

The rolling back of Roe v. Wade in America creates a nervous system survival state as it says that the most powerful nation in the world does not believe in a woman or birthing person's right to choose whether or not they go ahead with a pregnancy. While this is a law that impacts American citizens, it speaks to the broader systemic issue of a woman or birthing person's autonomy, control over their bodies, and their ability to make choices about their future.

When our autonomy is threatened, it can create a chronic state of stress, keeping us in a state of hyperarousal. The examples I have shared demonstrate the way our systems threaten the safety of women and groups that are marginalized. Needless to say, the impact is more pervasive when your womanhood intersects with another identity that is marginalized, such as being a Black woman with a disability. It also highlights the fragility of democracy and how it can be dominated by men with power. Finally, it reminds us that global issues are our issues.

> *'I am not free while any woman is unfree, even when her shackles are very different from my own.'*
>
> **Audre Lorde**

Living in a world where women's fundamental rights are disputed or under threat contributes to a chronic state of stress or anxiety which will automatically trigger our survival response. This has adverse effects on mental and physical health.

In Western society, the definition of success is often defined by career progression, financial stability, and continuous self-improvement; it is not uncommon for people to refer to themselves as a 'work in progress.' This mindset, fueled by societal expectations, the media, and cultural norms, creates a culture of urgency and pressure. Each goal or task becomes a 'threat' that needs to be overcome for survival. The business coaching world is full of messages about being stuck at income brackets. This has led to me being on coaching calls where women have been visibly distressed at 'being stuck' at £50,000 per month, the equivalent of £600,000 per year, forgetting that the national average income in the UK is less than what they are frustrated by making in a month. The nervous system doesn't differentiate between a physical threat and a psychological one – in both cases, it responds by preparing the body for action, leading to heightened stress levels. As far as the nervous system is concerned, distress is distress, whether it is caused by 'only' making £50,000 per month or the distress of genuine financial insecurity.

For women, the pressure to be successful is often compounded by societal norms and expectations in relation to domestic work and caregiving. Women still shoulder a disproportionate share of household chores, emotional labor, and caregiving tasks. This is often referred to as the 'second shift.' After coming home from a day of paid work, women often have another round of unpaid work to do. The need to manage this balancing act between professional and personal life can create a constant state of stress, again triggering the survival state in the nervous system.

The societal pressure to be a good mother, a good partner, as well as a successful professional, places conflicting demands on women, which inevitably leads to feelings of shame, inadequacy, and failure, creating an enduring stress response that we normalize. This will often manifest through stress-related symptoms such as insomnia, anxiety, depression, and other physical and mental health problems. Our society creates an environment where we ignore these signals from our bodies as we don't want to be seen as making a fuss or being needy. This, combined with fluctuating hormones due to our menstrual cycles, and the significant changes we encounter in perimenopause and menopause, means that women are constantly working too much just to survive.

BEFRIENDING OUR BIOLOGY

Our biology is not designed for constant threat and chronic stress. We are beings that require safety, rest, pleasure, and play. These are not luxuries or indulgences, but essential components of a healthy life, necessary for us to truly thrive. This is why sharing this knowledge is so important to me. Understanding that our struggles are not personal failings, but reflections of a society that often operates in a manner contrary to our biological needs, can empower us to create meaningful, sustainable change.

Befriending our biology can support us to advocate for ourselves and others. With knowledge, we can begin to question and challenge the societal norms that perpetuate chronic stress and encourage an unhealthy activation of our survival states as if it's normal. We can initiate conversations around creating work that supports us to live well, mental health support, and social reform. Instead of fighting against systemic oppressions that continually place us in a state of fight or flight, we can begin to create systems that support human flourishing.

Equipped with the knowledge of our survival states and the understanding of our societal conditioning, we can begin to heal ourselves and reshape society. By championing safety, rest, pleasure, and play, we can create a world where our biological needs are not just acknowledged but prioritized. A world where survival states are temporary responses, not perpetual states of being. A world where we do not merely survive, but thrive.

THE AUTONOMIC LADDER

I would like to focus on the way our everyday ordinary life triggers signs of danger and glimmers of safety. My aim is to demonstrate how what we cognitively process as normal impacts us on a somatic level and how this shapes our lived experiences.

When we think about our fight, flight, or freeze response being activated, we generally think about it in the context of an event that evokes explicit fear, such as a disagreement, a loud bang, when we see a toddler running toward a pond in a park, or a car that looks like it's not going to stop while we're on the crossing.

When we can attune to the signals from our bodies, we can start to identify where we are on the 'autonomic ladder.' The ladder metaphor is used to illustrate the hierarchy of the ANS (Autonomic Nervous System); it often focuses on the sympathetic and parasympathetic systems and includes a third rung representing a socially engaged state called ventral, as per Stephen Porges's Polyvagal Theory.[8]

Here is a simplified description of the ladder:

- Top of the Ladder – Ventral Vagal State (Parasympathetic Dominance):

  ~ This part of the ladder is 200 million years old.

  ~ It is often considered the optimal state, where we feel safe and social, otherwise known as normal. This state is characterized by feelings of calm, relaxation, and social engagement. The body's rest, digest, and social engagement functions are predominant here.

- Middle of the Ladder – Sympathetic State:

  ~ This part of the ladder is 400 million years old.

  ~ This is our body's response to stress or danger, often referred to as the 'fight-or-flight' response. Here, the heart rate increases, pupils dilate, and adrenaline is released to prepare the body for action.

  ~ Under normal, healthy conditions our sympathetic nervous system is like a starter motor that gets us going.

- Bottom of the Ladder – Dorsal Vagal State (Extreme Parasympathetic Dominance):

  ~ This is the oldest part of the ladder at 500 million years old.

~   This is the body's response to extreme stress or perceived life threat, often referred to as the freeze or shut-down response. It is characterized by feelings of disconnection, numbness, and immobilization. The function of dorsal state is to immobilize and disconnect – aka, hide.

These systems are organized in a hierarchy in the sense that one system will dominate over the other depending on the body's needs. In a situation of rest and relaxation, the ventral state takes precedence. In a situation of stress or danger, the dorsal or sympathetic state dominates. However, we are moving between these states all the time as the sympathetic system and parasympathetic systems support our bodies to function. As such, I prefer to use waves to illustrate the hierarchy as under normal conditions we ebb and flow between states throughout the day. This also helps my clients to refrain from viewing ventral as positive and superior to the other states, which we tend to view as negative. This helps reduce instances of them labeling themselves 'wrong' when they are not in a ventral state.

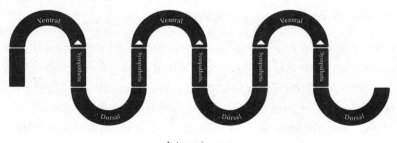

Autonomic waves

Each branch of the ANS has a hierarchy of effects on different organs. For example, when the sympathetic system is activated, it prioritizes increasing heart rate and blood pressure, dilating the pupils, and slowing digestion. When our safety is threatened these are the biological states that enable us to stand up for ourselves in the face of danger (fight) or run from it (flight). In day-to-day life it enables us to get going and take action; for example, inhaling deeply before walking into a meeting.

The parasympathetic system, when activated, prioritizes slowing heart rate, constricting pupils, and increasing digestion. In a survival dorsal state that may look like hiding from danger when you're unable to fight or flee. In day-to-day life it may look like avoiding eye contact and making yourself small, so you don't get called on in a meeting. In a ventral state, the parasympathetic system allows us to be risk-aware rather than risk-averse, we feel safe and grounded. It doesn't mean that everything is positive, but we have greater resilience, view challenges as part of life, and have the capacity to navigate them.

This hierarchy allows the body to allocate its resources effectively and efficiently in response to different demands. Our need to survive will always override our desire to thrive; therefore, when we feel threatened our bodies will work overtime to protect us. However, with this knowledge, we can begin to bring conscious awareness to the way we respond to our reactions.

For example, instead of spiraling into feeling overwhelmed before you say no, state a need, or initiate a challenging conversation, you can remind yourself that you're nervous, acknowledge that you're not about to die, and engage in a behavior that will help you feel a commensurate level of stress rather than be overwhelmed. Before a presentation or sales pitch, I'll dance to move and release excess energy. It will also help me to feel better. Then I state three things I'm grateful for and three ways my work can add value. This helps to settle my nerves, put things in perspective, and make me feel good about what I'm about to do. I also use this strategy when I'm going to have a difficult conversation with someone I care about. This helps me embark on the conversation from a place of curiosity and compassion instead of fear and judgement. There are also times when my sympathetic nervous system needs to be activated, so I'll listen to LL Cool J's 'Mama Said Knock You Out' or Dizzee Rascal's 'Stop Dat.' These tracks are guaranteed to help me step into my warrior energy and stand up for myself and my beliefs.

Our nervous system is designed to be flexible so that we can navigate this ladder with ease. Knowing how to partner with your nervous system states and tend to them is vital.

Profile Map

I did a training course by Deb Dana called 'The Foundations of Polyvagal Informed Practice' *(see page 259)*. It was a six-month training program to become a Polyvagal Informed Practitioner. During this training, we were taught how to create a 'profile map' to help our clients understand the landscape of their nervous system.

I have shared this with groups and with individuals and the effect is profound as people are able to understand themselves in a manner that is compassionate and supportive rather than chastising and coercive.

For this exercise, we are going to focus on the ventral, survival sympathetic, and dorsal states.

You will need three blank sheets of paper and some colored pens or pencils.

Before we go into the exercise, I invite you to consider what you're like in a ventral state. I liken this state to feeling 'normal;' you're grounded, present, and optimistic. Consequently, you experience challenges as a part of life you have the capacity to navigate.

Now I invite you to think about when you're scared, tired, or stressed. What is your default survival state? For example, you have worked hard to create a presentation you're proud of. Forty-eight hours before your presentation your laptop breaks down, deleting your presentation. Do you fight, flee, freeze, or fawn?

When someone you care about continuously disregards your boundary, which survival state do you default to?

When you have hurt someone's feelings what is your nervous system reaction?

Mapping Ventral

1. Write down words you associate with being in a ventral state.

2. If ventral was a type of weather, what would it be? Draw this on your paper.

3. Describe your behavior when you're in a ventral state.

4. What colors do you associate with ventral?

5. What sort of events, people, places, experiences, and things help you tap into ventral?

6. If ventral was energy, what type of energy would it be?

7. Anything else?

Mapping Survival Sympathetic

I have used the term 'survival sympathetic' as this branch of the nervous system is not just about survival. It supports several necessary functions that enable us to live our lives. For this exercise, the focus is on the experience of our survival responses.

1. Write down words you associate with being in a survival sympathetic state.

2. If survival sympathetic was a type of weather, what would it be? Draw this on your paper.

3. Describe your behavior when you're in a survival sympathetic state.

4. What colors do you associate with a survival sympathetic state?

5. What sort of events, people, places, experiences, and things trigger a survival sympathetic state for you?

6. If survival sympathetic was energy, what type of energy would it be?

7. Anything else?

Mapping Dorsal

1. Write down words you associate with being in dorsal state.

2. If the dorsal state was a type of weather, what would it be? Draw this on your paper.

3. Describe your behavior when you're in a survival dorsal state.

4. What colors do you associate with dorsal state?

5. What sort of events, people, places, experiences, and things trigger dorsal state for you?

6. If dorsal state was energy, what type of energy would it be?

7. Anything else?

Were there any common threads in your responses? For example, it's not uncommon to notice that the same person or people may activate our ventral and survival states – family members, friends, and partners often do this.

When our bodies detect danger we automatically, autonomically go into a survival state. This happens below the level of consciousness. We have no control over our biological reactions. However, we can learn how to respond and, over time, how to preempt our biological responses. This builds self-trust and self-worth, and it is from this place that we manifest.

Your answers to question 5 in Mapping Ventral are your key resources for developing a true sense of what's normal and healthy for you, rather than what you've been conditioned to normalize (such as constant low-level anxiety). These are the activities, foods, people, and practices that help you to feel relaxed and grounded. Some will be as simple as a walk in the park or taking some slow, easy breaths. For introverts, time alone is essential for regulating the nervous system, while for extroverts, socializing is a tonic. Become aware of what works for you.

///

BUILDING SELF-AWARENESS

Our bodies will give us subtle, early signs of nervous system changes or distress, and with practice we can become better at reading these signals. We begin to sense when our body is saying no while our conditioning is telling us to say yes. We become more aligned with our gut feelings or instinct. We feel all our feelings and allow them to flow through us, rather than burying them deep inside.

Here are some of the incredible senses we have to help us build this embodied awareness:

Proprioception

Our sense of proprioception enables us to perceive the position and movement of our bodies, even without looking at them. You can try this now if it is safe for you to do so. Close your eyes and touch the tip of your nose with your right index finger. Your sense of proprioception allowed you to do that. You were able to do it by processing a variety of sensory information that you detected with the nerve receptors in your body, including in the muscles, joints, and skin.

You did not need to think about this – you just did it – but take a moment to think about the fact that you processed numerous pieces of sensory information that you detected with the nerve receptors in your body. Aren't you amazing? If you're not amazed by that, I don't know what to tell you.

This sense is crucial for all sorts of everyday activities, such as walking, eating, and virtually any action that requires control of our limbs. It's also very important in sports and other physical activities where precise control of body positioning and movement is required.

Interoception

Interoception is the sense of the internal state of the body. It's how you understand and feel what's going on inside you. This can include feelings of hunger or fullness, the need to go to the bathroom, heart rate, and even the sensation of an emotion.

Interoceptive signals are detected by receptors within the body that monitor various physiological parameters, such as blood pressure, body temperature, pH balance, glucose levels, and more. This information is communicated to the brain, where it's integrated and processed, resulting in perceptions like hunger, thirst, temperature, pain, and other internal sensations.

Interoception plays a key role in homeostasis (maintaining a stable internal environment in the body), as well as emotional experiences and self-awareness. Some research even suggests that a heightened focus on interoception may contribute to conditions like anxiety, depression, eating disorders, and others.

Like other sensory systems, interoception can vary greatly from person to person. Some people may have a heightened sense of their internal state, while others may be less aware of their internal sensations. This variability can have significant implications for physical and mental health, behavior, and overall well-being.

Exteroception

Exteroception is the sensory perception of the environment outside of the body. This involves senses that receive and process information from the external world, helping us interact and respond appropriately to our surroundings. The main exteroceptive senses include:

- **Vision:** This allows us to perceive light, colors, shapes, distances, and movement.

- **Hearing:** This allows us to perceive sound, including pitch, volume, and direction.

- **Smell:** This allows us to perceive various odors.

- **Taste:** This allows us to perceive different flavors.

- **Touch:** This allows us to perceive pressure, vibration, temperature, and sensations on the skin, such as itching or pain.

These senses play a vital role in our day-to-day interactions with the world around us. They help us to understand our environment, navigate through it, and communicate with others.

In comparison, interoception and proprioception are considered as 'internal' senses, as they involve perceiving the state and movement of the body itself rather than the external world.

Practice Pause

P.I.E. Body Scan

- Start by finding a comfortable position. This may be sitting, lying down, or even standing. Take a moment to tune into your body and allow yourself to be guided by it. If it feels good and safe to do so, allow your eyes to gently close. If not, softly gaze at something in the distance so you can focus on yourself and your internal experience.

- We'll begin with exteroception, our perception of the environment around us. Take a moment to notice the feel of the air against your skin. Is it cool or warm? Notice the clothes against your body, the weight of your body against the chair or floor. Tune into the sounds that you can hear. They might be close by or far away. There is no need to listen to them, just notice the sounds around you.

- Now, we'll explore proprioception, the awareness of our bodies that doesn't need sight. Keeping your eyes closed, bring your attention to your body. Sense the position of your limbs. Can you feel where your hands are resting? Can you sense the position of your feet? Try moving your fingers or toes slightly. Note how you know they're moving without needing to look at them.

- Finally, let's focus on interoception, the awareness of our .internal body state. Shift your attention to your breath. You don't need to change your breathing. Simply notice it. Feel the rise and fall of your chest or belly. Maybe you can feel your heart beating in your chest or pulse throbbing in your fingertips. Pay attention to any other sensations – feelings of hunger or fullness, tension, or relaxation.

- Now, let's bring this together. Shift your attention to the world around you. Sense your body's position in space, and the internal sensations. Feel the harmony of these three senses, working together to give you a full perception of your existence.

- Let's take a deep breath in, holding this integrated awareness, and slowly let it out. When you're ready, shift your attention to the connection between your skin and whatever you're sitting, standing, or lying on to bring this practice to a gentle close. When you're ready, slowly allow your eyes to open and thank yourself for this moment.

You can access the audio version of this practice online *(see page 259)* or in the audiobook.

CO-REGULATION

In the story of human evolution, there's a theme that keeps showing up: our need for connection and belonging. It provides us with the reassuring feeling of being understood, loved, and cared for. It's also about a natural process that helps us understand ourselves and the world around us. This process is called 'co-regulation.'

Co-regulation is like a dance between two people. It's not a dance you see with your eyes, but one you feel – a rhythm, melody, and movement experienced by your nervous system and sensed by the nervous systems of others. It's the cornerstone of our relationships, helping us to adjust to our needs and the world around us.

When we were infants, our parents/caregivers helped us learn this dance. They were the barometer by which we measured how to engage with the world. The calming voice of a parent or carer, their gentle touch, and their peaceful presence were things that helped us learn how to regulate our emotions and physical responses. This dance of connection taught us how to manage our 'fight-or-flight' (survival) responses and our 'rest-and-digest' (connection) activities.

The symbiotic nature of these relationships means that the same connection that enables us to co-regulate can also lead to what's known as 'co-dysregulation'. This happens when we mirror the emotional state of another person, but instead of creating harmony, it amplifies stress or distress. For instance, if someone around us is anxious, we might start to feel anxious, too. I can feel very anxious when I'm running late, and my daughter will ask me to keep my 'anxious vibes' to myself as she can sense my anxiety levels even when I'm trying to keep them contained. The saying 'misery loves company' is a cliché for a reason. Thankfully, I have also modeled personal boundaries, so my daughter can differentiate her feelings from mine.

Co-dysregulation can be especially challenging in situations where social pressures and societal norms push us to absorb the emotional states of others, sometimes at the expense of our own well-being. This is evidenced in the construct of traditional gender roles. For example, in a society that conditions women to please people, it is not uncommon for women with clear boundaries to be seen as selfish or inconsiderate if they do not absorb the emotional states of others.

Co-regulation teaches us how to self-regulate; we are not born with this skill. Although this is hardwired into our programming from an early age, we can create new wiring to counteract the old. The 'hardwire' will always be present but, with practice, we can utilize the new wiring to help us make healthier choices.

SELF-REGULATION

Self-regulation is our ability to manage our emotions and make conscious choices about the way we respond to the world around us. It enables us to make choices that support connection and uphold our values. For example, choosing not to chase the car that overtook you badly so you can tell the driver that they are a reckless dickhead. Self-regulation is an essential skill for us to manage the complexity of living in a manner that is grounded and adaptable (not 'mal-adaptable').

It would be remiss to believe we can exist independently, be totally self-made or self-reliant. Just like the intricate mycelium network underground that enriches and interconnects all life on Earth, the fabric of our human nature also thrives on connection. It is a biological need. Co-regulation and co-dysregulation forms the invisible network that binds us all together. The shape of this interwoven network is profoundly influenced by the systems that dominate our lives. Our nervous system reflects the system in which we live.

Consequently, the oppressive trinity of capitalism, patriarchy, and white supremacy disrupts our human nature. These systems of power threaten our safety, sending our bodies signals of danger and normalizing co-dysregulation. Just look at how we are conditioned to constantly compare ourselves with others on social media, for example, or at the school gate.

When we notice what's happening inside us, instead of shutting it down we can learn to regulate ourselves. Understanding how oppressive systems of power affect our ability to connect and tend to our emotions can help us be more understanding of and kind to ourselves and others. The level of vulnerability required for this makes it extremely challenging but our ability to adapt means that we have the capacity to unlearn harmful behaviors and relearn behaviors that will support the co-regulation necessary to create systems that respect our biological need for connection.

Authentic connection and self-regulation provide us with a level of safety that tells our sympathetic nervous system it can rest and activates our parasympathetic nervous system's state of rest and digest. It is from this place that we can allow ourselves to be seen as we are rather than the filtered versions we share when we feel unsafe. This level of connection feels like a sanctuary where you're welcome because of your flaws not despite them. My group coaching clients are always amazed that they connected with each other due to qualities they believed to be weird. The original meaning of the word weird is 'having the power to control destiny' – give me weird all day long!

This level of connection is deep and wide enough to hold vulnerable conversations and the most satisfying joy. These spaces allow our shoulders to relax, our jaws to unclench, and our stomachs to soften. They connect us, nervous system to nervous system, and show us that our differences are what makes us an ecosystem. This enables us to stop projecting societal norms that cause us harm and explore how we can take responsibility for creating cultures that are socially just and communities of care.

Your body is the most spiritual place on this planet.

Containing Earth and Heaven. Soil and stardust.

Created in darkness, born into light.

A beginner in water, mastering land.

An embodiment of evolution defying logic and time.

You were not birthed to merely toil and die.

Wonderfully and fearfully made, a reflection of twinkles in the sky.

Your organs reverberate with the universe's sacred echo.

Within your nervous system, the melody of the cosmos is bestowed.

You are a splendor, a miracle for true.

All of this nestled in the wonder that is you.

'There is more wisdom in your body than
in your deepest philosophy.'
Friedrich Nietzsche

Joy Practice

Following on from Chapter 2, this joy practice is singing!

- Singing is an effective stress reliever because it releases endorphins, which are chemicals that make us feel good. It tells your nervous system you're safe, as you would not be singing if you were in danger. Singing also stimulates the vagus nerve. This nerve plays a vital role in our autonomic functions such as our breathing and heart rate. It is also a major component of the PNS, which is why singing soothes fractious babies.

- Singing with others promotes a sense of community and connectedness, as the group is singing from the same hymn sheet (sorry, I couldn't resist!) and engaging in a unifying activity.

- The way we breathe when we are singing tends to be controlled, rhythmic, and measured, which has a calming effect.

- And finally, neuroscience has found that our dopamine center is very active when we listen to happy music. I think that's a good reason to listen to 'Happy' by Pharrell Williams.

I invite you to find your finest hairbrush and sing along to one of your favorite tracks. Once you're done, note if there's a difference in how you felt before and after.

//

Dear One,

It's time to awaken from your slumber.

To shake off the mask of who you've become.

You are a child of the Divine, defying
odds that baffle logic and time.

The facade you've learned to wear stifles your
energy, creating a rupture only you can repair.

For this, you must become both your steward
and your guide so you may tend to your inner
landscape and clear the path home.

Rise from your slumber – let today be the day!

Freedom awaits – your heart knows the way.

CHAPTER 4

MEETING THE REAL YOU

'Embodiment is the practice of attending to your sensations. Awareness of your body serves as a guiding compass to help you feel more in charge of the course of your life. Somatic awareness provides a foundation for empathy, helps you make healthy decisions, and gives important feedback about your relationships with others. Embodiment in somatic psychology applies mindfulness and movement practices to awaken body awareness as a tool for healing.'

Dr. Arielle Schwartz

On that note, I'd like to share that as I write about embracing the real you, I'm struggling with being the real me – the need to prove myself and my knowledge by 'sounding clever' is very strong!

My ongoing journey of self-awareness has allowed me to practice self-compassion. Some of the ways I do this include: going for 'beauty walks,' during which I pay attention to the splendor of my surroundings; listening to African gospel music; and sitting on my pink contemplation chair, inviting fear to join me. This time, I felt the fear move from my chest to my lap. As it rested there, my fear told me I'm scared to enjoy this process, as I have a core belief that I must struggle – even though I know my best work comes from joy. This narrative – that success is precipitated by struggle – makes anything that doesn't require grit and grind feel like cheating, as I haven't 'worked hard enough.' My body tries to shield me from the allure of pleasure by sowing seeds of doubt that strengthen my inclination toward hardship and struggle.

I'm sharing this to highlight how easy it is to disconnect from our embodied experience when we are used to living in survival mode and how this can fuel toxic productivity addiction. The thing is, toxic productivity gets results, and anxiety can be an effective motivational tool. My procrastination is always 'productive.' On this occasion it led to me creating a new coaching program, developing and launching my membership community 'The Life & Business

Sanctuary', planning a live event, and a decluttering session – but it came at the cost of sacrificing my joy and long-term satisfaction for instant gratification.

As part of my compassion practice, I forgave the part of me that was fearful by moving my body while I recited the Ho'oponopono prayer to chill house music – healing but make it fun. I'll share the forgiveness practice later in this chapter – chill house is optional! During my practice, the sensations in my body (interoception) invited me to move in a manner that felt forgiving, tender, and kind. It involved lots of bowing, chest opening, and gentle touch. I rarely cry but, on this occasion, a few tears flowed. I ended this practice with a bath and early night – I slept like a newborn.

Giving myself grace is possible because I feel safe enough to connect with the feeling of my sensations and I know my recovery from toxic productivity addiction is a lifelong endeavor – much like a person addicted to chemical substances will always be in recovery. On the surface, this may sound bleak, but it isn't. It's radical self-acceptance and befriending the real me.

Thank you for witnessing me! Now it's your turn.

Meeting the real you enables you to meet yourself where you are rather than judging yourself according to where you think you *should* be. It begins with self-forgiveness, followed by self-compassion, leading towards self-acceptance.

A Moment of Connection

Sit with your feet flat on the floor. As you exhale, use the skill of proprioception to feel the soles of your feet connecting with the floor beneath you. Then pay attention to where your body connects with what you're sitting on. With each exhale, allow your body to soften. Note how it feels heavier. Whatever you're sitting on and whatever surface your feet are resting on is being supported by the Earth. Therefore, *you* are supported by the Earth. Imagine the Earth's warm energy traveling through the soles of your feet and throughout your body. Feel the warm Earth energy traveling through your body, offering you support. On each exhale, invite yourself to soften a little more. Rest and allow yourself to feel held.

The aim is for you to come back into your body and feel connected. The more often you do this connection exercise the more you'll build an internal feeling of support.

//

So, who is the real you and how do you begin to meet her?

The oppressive trinity of white supremacy, patriarchy, and capitalism forms tightly woven threads throughout the tapestry of our lives, binding us all with common themes. For women, these threads create fabrics that bind us tightly, and these binds are exacerbated for women of color, particularly Black women, who are at the intersection of misogyny *and* anti-Black racism. As these systems of oppression are centuries old, their effect is intergenerational – conditions passed down from generation to generation through culture, tradition, and DNA. These conditions form a psychological contract, which creates covert 'rules' that underpin the overt ones. For example, the overt rule that women are natural caretakers sets up the covert rule that creates an environment where it's believed that women taking responsibility for much of the emotional and domestic labor in their families is their duty. The reward? Being called selfless.

Or when it's assumed that female staff members will organize office social events. Or when women believe that tolerating relationships where their emotional needs are neglected is 'just how it is.' On the social media app TikTok, there are countless videos of women calling out the 'weaponized incompetence' of men in heterosexual relationships. For example, using stereotypes to avoid responsibility, such as women are better at multitasking; men don't clean as well as women; men don't remember significant events like birthdays or anniversaries; and so on. They don't have to while we live up to stereotypes. At best, many men play on this and at worst, don't even try. So, the responsibility falls to women, who cope by over-functioning. For example, not doing the dishes properly so the women in their lives get pissed off and decide that it's better for them to handle this chore because the man 'can't' – hello patriarchy!

This oppressive system includes men believing that women being unhappy in relationships is normal. A writer called Shar Henley dubbed this the 'tolerable level of permanent unhappiness' and it went viral. Let's pause here for a moment. A tolerable level of permanent unhappiness – how does this land with you?

My family is from the Krio ethnic group in Sierra Leone. There is a Krio saying: 'Bad man Bɛtɛ pas emhti os' – a bad man is better than an empty house. It's that old adage again, isn't it – 'Better the devil you know'? It even became a pop song by Kylie Minogue in 1990! Popular music really did a number on us all. I will not mention RnB... OK, I will – Boyz II Men's 'End of the Road' and an honorable mention for Lisa Stansfield's 'All Woman.' Please google the lyrics. I shudder to think about how popular music has informed the psychological contract of romantic relationships.

I share this as a reminder that many of the choices we make are the result of ingrained conditioning that permeates society from the pop charts to boardrooms, to how the dishwasher is loaded.

In this environment, connecting to who you are and acknowledging your true self and your needs feels unsafe – because when you do, you're faced with two options: either experience the short-term pain of making changes that may include losing some relationships or consciously choose the ongoing pain of assisting in your own oppression and lose yourself – to me, that's the worst kind of betrayal.

The little girl inside me learned to avoid disappointment by disappointing herself first – for example, suppressing her aspirations, as she was accustomed to being met with doubt. Maybe the little girl inside you became adept at judging herself harshly because her caregivers were overtly focused on her achieving top marks and being 'good' so she could live their unlived lives. Or maybe she learned to manage the chaos of her home environment by squashing down her needs. Maybe that little girl found that she could not have needs that inconvenienced others because a sibling or parent had needs that overshadowed everything. These responses were childhood adaptations – coping strategies to survive caregivers who were unable to meet your needs when you were little. Please do not repeat these patterns. You are your caregiver now.

> *'The greatest burden a child must bear*
> *is the unlived life of its parents.'*
> Carl Jung

In Chapter 1, I set out how we got here. Chapter 2 provided an insight as to how you maladapted to cope with systems of oppression that inform our whole lives. Chapter 3 highlighted the ways our everyday experiences can send us signs of danger that activate our survival responses. It also helped you to identify signs of safety so that you can become risk-aware rather than risk-averse. This paved the way for meeting the real you.

BREAKING FREE OF OLD PATTERNS

You had to make adaptations so you could cope, but to break free of the pattern of survival and find your joy you need to meet the real you so you can embody her fully. The you that has been sending signals via the feelings you have learned to label as 'bad' or 'negative,' such as rage, resentment, frustration, and envy. When you're able to meet these parts of yourself with tenderness, you'll also meet the you that has been sending you signals via the joy, pleasure, satisfaction, and contentment you have been taught to minimize in case it makes you lose your 'edge.' Feelings you have been taught are rewards for reaching a target that seems to move into the distance as soon as you get close, making it impossible to feel worthy of savoring your accomplishments.

This is not your fault. It is by design. The good news is you have the power to create a new design. However, doing so requires a level of vulnerability that can feel harrowing at first. It's important not to confuse this pain of labor – which comes with all growth and change – with the pain of endless struggle. At the end of this labor, you'll discover the freedom to grow into someone who can choose – rather than abandon yourself. It's wiser to endure this finite pain than to settle for the lifelong, dull ache of being a stranger to yourself just to gain and retain acceptance from people and systems that are unable or unwilling to see your true beauty. The cultural conditioning you had to adapt to shaped you for survival, but you deserve to thrive. You deserve joy. It's time to break free, do the work, and meet the real you.

This work is trauma healing. It's biological, emotional, psychological, and spiritual. It's political, racial, and historical. It imprints your DNA, and the depth of this imprint matches the depth of your hue. This imprint concerns epigenetics, which we'll look at below. This work also requires focus and radical responsibility because it is so complex, your need for certainty will be shaken to its core and your nervous system may mistake this for serious danger. You'll need to reassure yourself with a level of compassion and kindness that could make you feel weak – but it's not weakness. It's like the pain of 'shredding' muscles that precedes their growth and repair. With care and time, the pain will pass, but the process must continue if you want to maintain your gains.

HOW SYSTEMS SUPPRESS YOUR DNA

I love a bit of science, so let's talk a little more about epigenetics. The Centers for Disease Control and Prevention (CDC) in the USA defines epigenetics as the 'study of how your behaviors and environment can cause changes that affect the way your genes work.'[1]

These things can act like a remote control for our DNA, switching genes on or off, akin to adjusting a TV's volume, channel, or screen display. If the remote control is faulty, it can send incorrect commands to the TV and what you see, hear, and experience on the screen doesn't match the button you pressed on the remote.

Epigenetic change is influenced by our lifestyle, experiences, and surroundings, impacting reactions to stimuli, growth, and health. It significantly influences our behavior. So, just like the faulty TV remote, the effects of persistent trauma in your family history are known to affect the way you might view, process, and respond to events in your own life.

Systemic oppression leaves marks on our DNA, potentially affecting future generations. This can lead to hypervigilance, people-pleasing behaviors, and overworking, to name a few. It's not exclusive to those of African descent, but looking at epigenetics did lead me to consider how it might impact the emotional well-being of a British-born daughter of Caribbean parents due to exposure to white supremacy.

My own family history includes facing overt racial discrimination. My grandparents, arriving in the UK, were met with signs reading 'No Irish, no Blacks, no dogs.' This, coupled with my granddad's childhood experiences in colonial Sierra Leone, may have influenced my DNA, shaping the 'strong Black woman' archetype I embody.

But it's not just about struggle. My ancestors also imprinted resilience, hope, fortitude, optimism, and courage. Epigenetic change transmits information across generations, encompassing both post-traumatic stress and post-traumatic growth. Ultimately, it's a wellspring we can all draw from as we embark on discovering our true selves.

GOING BENEATH THE SURFACE

Meeting the real you can feel discombobulating, especially after a lifetime of being taught to live for others and equating it with being 'good.' During a coaching session, one of my clients was so exhausted that she became tearful. It wasn't just about needing sleep. She required all seven types of rest, as outlined by Dr Saundra Dalton-Smith *(see page 157)*. Some of my clients' tears were due to her realizing that her life revolved around pleasing others. This began in childhood when she felt the duty to be the embodiment of the safety and better life her grandparents had sought as refugees in the UK.

This adaptation became a maladaptation in adulthood as she prioritized being seen as a 'good person,' always appeasing others to her own detriment. As an adult, she juggled being a good wife, mother, daughter, businessperson, and friend. Her entire life focused on ensuring others were content, leaving little room for understanding what truly satisfied her.

As I coached her so she could identify how she could resource herself and recover from exhaustion, my client struggled to pinpoint anything unrelated to what she could do for others. Her family and work were at the center of her life, and she was on the periphery. Activities like having fun, engaging in creative pursuits without a specific purpose, or doing things that brought her joy and delight seemed foreign to her.

This realization left her feeling lost – her self-concept was based on who she was for others. She had become a stranger to herself, and the system of capitalism, with its promotion of costly experiences like retreats and spa days, limited her self-care to occasional indulgences instead of a low-cost (or free) daily practice.

We've been conditioned to believe that self-care can be found in occasional and extravagant experiences. We often overlook the importance of the small things in our lives. Truly nourishing self-care comes from the micro-actions we take moment by moment, day by day. It's in the rituals and routines we weave into the fabric of our daily lives.

As I reminded my client of the power of micro-activities and practices, her face lit up as she remembered her love for swimming. This was her start and she agreed to go for a weekly swim without her children. I highlighted that over the period of a year that weekly swim becomes 52 swims! I also asked her to imagine the positive role model she would become for her family.

Micro-habits have a compounding effect. For example, if you wanted to increase your flexibility you would stretch regularly. You wouldn't stretch all day for three days and never again then expect the results you desire. You'd also maintain a regular practice to sustain your flexibility. We like the idea of intense experiences because there's no ongoing commitment or need to make meaningful change – we just need to endure the intensity. And intense experiences are not the same as persistent changes that reshape your life.

In our culture of overconsumption and complexity, we forget that ordinary moments of joy, restoration, and self-connection are powerful. This power is not dominant and coercive, it is inspirational and wholesome. Our conditioning tells us that prioritizing ourselves is selfish, as it assumes we are prioritizing ourselves above others. That is not the case. It serves as a reminder that you are a priority, too. Meeting the real you and making micro-choices that nourish you enables you to become your own best friend. It is also a radical stand against systems that thrive on our depletion and lack of discernment.

Instead of running on autopilot, we can make powerful choices about how we use our energy (which we explore in the next chapter on being naturally productive), enabling us to have the courage necessary to question the status quo and advocate for meaningful change. This is how we restore our agency.

VALIDATING ALL OF YOU

Meeting the real you is hard because so many of our experiences in our formative years were invalidated. We may have hurt ourselves and been told not to cry, been upset and told not to make a fuss. Perhaps we told the truth and were told 'No one likes a telltale.' Whichever the case, our reality was denied by often well-meaning adults. How many of us have been conditioned to equate ignoring pain with 'being brave'?

Whether intended or not, these experiences invalidated our experiences and caused us to form the habit of second-guessing ourselves. As such, we learned to question whether how we feel is real or justified.

Exercise

Consider a low-level situation where your reality was invalidated by a parent, caregiver, or educational professional.

NB: Please stick to a low-level situation. This is intended to be a gentle exercise, not an intense experience. Remember – emotional safety over intensity, always! There is a lot to be gained by gentleness.

Reflect on this situation as you are now and answer the following in your journal:

- What type of response would have felt supportive?

- What type of language would have felt supportive?

- What tone of voice would have felt welcoming and told you that your experience was valid?

- What action would you have liked to see?

- How might this have made you feel?

Your responses are likely to be what you need to feel validated, seen, heard, and held now.

I invite you to revisit what you have written and read it slowly. Consider how you can incorporate some of your responses day-to-day so that you can begin to back yourself. Remember, every version of you – past, present, and future – is within you right now. Self-validation in the present travels through time, healing the past and paving the way for the future.

Now put your left hand on your chest and your right hand on your stomach. Allow your stomach to soften, take a deep breath in and a deep breath out, then read the following:

- Although I cannot go back in time to right wrongs, I can remain present and validate myself now.

- Validating myself now takes care of my inner child and helps me deepen my self-trust.

- I take full responsibility for every version of me, knowing that this is a time-traveling radical act of deep self-love.

And so it is.

///

EMBODIMENT IS SELF-AWARENESS

In removing the facade and meeting the real you, you might find that you're messier and more chaotic than the woman you have learned to show the world. You might be more opinionated or like to sit quietly in contemplation. You might be desperate for some quality, nourishing rest, or yearning for adventures, such as hiking or a change of career. All of this is normal and getting to know these parts of yourself cannot be rushed. This phase requires acceptance and trust. The practices throughout this book will assist in rebuilding self-trust; the process is gentle and consistent. The more frequently you engage in the practices, the more effective they'll be. Trust is constructed over time and shaped by experience. It's a natural process, like summer transitioning to autumn. It cannot be forced.

You won't find the real you in your overworked, overstretched, and possibly overwhelmed mind. You will find her when you lay your hands gently on your heart. You will find her when you take deep breaths that nourish the cells of your body.

Your body will tell you how you are, who you are, and what you need. You just have to ask and then be quiet and listen. Listen below the tiredness, below the awkwardness or self-consciousness, below the rules that feel like barriers. Listen into the cavernous depths because there you'll hear your soul. In order to meet ourselves, we need to allow ourselves to feel fully; this is what it is to be 'embodied.' Embodiment is a powerful form of awareness. This is how we get in touch with who we really are beneath all the 'shoulds' and pressures imposed upon us through our lives.

In a society where we have learned to detach from the intelligence of our bodies in the pursuit of productivity and being convenient, many of the women I work with start with little or no connection to their bodies. Some of them are so stuck in their freeze response that they find it hard to touch themselves. Their bodies become objects to be touched and enjoyed by others, but not by them. Self-touch is a big part of my work, but it can be very triggering when you feel like your body is a mystery waging war against you.

We also live in a society that tends to be ruled by the mind rather than the heart. Intellect over emotion. And yet, it was the heart that came first as our atoms and cells nestled in our mother's wombs binding together and shaping the person we would become. The heart, our first organ, came before the brain and told the world that we are alive. We experienced our beating hearts and a sense of aliveness before we had a brain to compute it. Our hearts preceded logic; our hearts led us first.

During a workshop I hosted about embodying your future, some participants expressed feeling anxious as they thought about the possibilities that lay ahead. I guided them to stay with their sensations for a moment and asked if what they were experiencing was anxiety or anticipation. In the beginning, anxiety and anticipation can feel very similar. If you're accustomed to defaulting to anxiety, it is easy to mistake one for the other. For example, a racing heartbeat, butterflies in the stomach, and shallow breathing. These sensations indicate that the sympathetic nervous system has been activated and can be mistaken for a survival response rather than a normal and healthy reaction to the anticipation of what's to come. Taking a pause to consider these sensations in the context of their current experience helped my clients be present rather than default to being fearful.

Many of the participants expressed a sense of relief when they realized that they were experiencing anticipation. This felt lighter, and rather than defaulting to fear, we came up with the term 'scarecited.' Sadly, we did not originate the term – I did a Google search, and it appears in several places. The point is that being 'scarecited' fuels curiosity and leaves enough space for courage, whereas anxiety tends to shut us down.

A LIGHT TOUCH

When your neck aches, what do you do? I'm hoping your response was to touch it. What does this touch do? Take the palm of your hand and gently lay it on your neck. How does that feel? How does your hand feel against your neck and how does your neck feel against the palm of your hand? I hope it feels warm and soothing, although I understand that it may not. Years ago, gentle touch for me was strictly for foreplay and sex. My frozen nervous system meant gentle touch for the sake of meaningful contact made me feel too vulnerable. After years of practice, I now enjoy consensual touch. My body immediately softens and is open to the intimacy of touch and it does not have to be related to sexual contact.

Here are some reasons why touch is important for humans:

- Touch is a fundamental human need. Our skill of neuroception (proprioception, interoception, and exteroception) shows that we are designed to respond to touch. Welcoming touch, in the form of hugs, a handshake, or a pat on the shoulder can demonstrate authenticity, connection, or empathy.

- Consensual touch has been shown to lower the stress hormone cortisol and increase the 'happy' hormone serotonin and the 'love' hormone oxytocin.[2] This lowers the heart rate and improves immune function. This is why loneliness – in cases where no consensual touch is present – should be considered a public health issue.

- Touch supports bonding. Think about the way babies are soothed when they are picked up. When my daughter was a baby, some of my friends commented on me picking her up and 'indulging' her when she cried. I will never leave a baby to cry if I can soothe them by picking them up and helping them to emotionally regulate.

- Touch also supports social bonding. In 2009, I was in tears in my boss's office, drowning in mum guilt and tricky social work cases. My boss offered me a tissue and briefly touched my arm. That millisecond of connection was so impactful that I'm telling you about it nearly 15 years later.

- Touch is an essential aspect of the human experience, and it plays a vital role in our physical, emotional, and social well-being. When we think of touch, we usually think about being touched by others. Soothing touch from others is important but I believe we overlook the power of self-touch. We have the power to provide ourselves with healing touch with the palms of our hands.

Feel-Good Hand Massage

Moisturize your hands slowly and intentionally. Pay attention to how it feels to touch and be touched simultaneously. Play with pressure and grip and take note of how different touch feels to you. Pay attention to what feels good; repeat and savor it.

The aim is to connect with yourself for who you are and how you feel so you start to experience yourself as pleasurable.

SELF-FORGIVENESS

We all carry memories of things we wish we'd done differently. In order to meet the real you, you need to forgive yourself. Forgive yourself for not knowing what you didn't know when you didn't know it and then forgive yourself for believing you should have known! We need to understand that we are products of our conditioning and that shaming ourselves for not knowing better is part of that conditioning. Self-forgiveness helps us to peel off a layer of conditioning and then heal the rawness that we feel once we see how badly we have been let down by adults and caregivers (who were also let down by adults and caregivers) because that is how the system was designed.

- Self-forgiveness clears the path and creates space for compassion, which in turn helps us see that the shame, guilt, and blame we have learned to carry does not belong to us.

- Self-forgiveness empowers us to meet ourselves with love and acceptance as and where we are.

- Self-forgiveness cleanses and atones, creating space for courage, healing, and growth, liberating us from the burden of past mistakes so they may become lessons in our journey of living.

Ho'oponopono

Ho'oponopono is an ancient Hawaiian spiritual practice that creates healing by gently and powerfully encouraging you to take radical loving responsibility for your thoughts, emotions, and actions. Ho'oponopono means to 'make right.' It's a practice of reconciliation and forgiveness. This could be forgiving yourself, your ancestors, family, friends, anyone, or anything you have a relationship with. This includes our planet.

This process can be a profound method of healing, as it works like a powerful adaptogen, repairing ruptures and restoring connection. It doesn't have to make sense if it can be felt by your heart.

It's a cleansing and atoning process. Cleansing and making right what is known and what is unknown. Cleansing and making right what was passed down by your ancestors. Cleansing and making right stories and patterns you hold inside that distort the truth of who you are.

Ho'oponopono allows you to begin to treat yourself the way you would treat a friend.

I came across Ho'oponopono on YouTube. The first time I did it, I felt a surge of sorrow that was so visceral I almost slammed my laptop shut. My reaction told me how much I needed this practice. Ho'oponopono is now part of my self-forgiveness practice.

This simple, yet deeply effective technique involves the repetition of four statements:

1. I'm sorry.

2. I love you.

3. Please forgive me.

4. Thank you.

How to Do It

- Sit comfortably.

- Allow your feet to connect with the ground beneath you. Feel into the soles of your feet against the ground and gently close your eyes.

- Slow your breathing down, making your exhale slightly longer than your inhale. Imagine your exhale traveling to the soles of your feet, deepening your connection with the ground. This tells your nervous system you're safe and activates your parasympathetic nervous system, which tells your brain you can relax.

- Put your left hand on your chest and your right hand over your navel. Feel the beat of your heart and the rise and fall of your chest and stomach.

- See if you can relax your body further with each exhale by inviting your body to smile. For example, inviting your hairline, inner ear, backs of your eyes, jaw, throat, shoulders, back, stomach, pelvic floor, and your joints to smile.

- As you invite your body to smile, turn your attention towards the sensations in your body.

- Then repeat these statements in your mind or out loud:

  » I'm sorry.

  » I love you.

  » Please forgive me.

  » Thank you.

- Repeat the phrases as many times as you need to.

- If any memories resurface or realizations occur, you do not have to do anything about them immediately. You can tell the memory that you'll be back or ask the memory or realization if you can sit with it for a moment. Wanting to 'do' or fix straight away is usually an unconscious attempt to numb and to shut down. Compassion is 'being with' the sensations, memories, and realizations so that you may understand rather than control.

- Once you have finished, move your attention to your ears while you keep your eyes closed. Listen to sounds in the distance, then listen a bit closer until you're hearing sounds in your immediate vicinity. Then wiggle your fingers and toes, thank yourself and the Hawaiian ancestors, then gently open your eyes.

- If you like, you can spend some time journaling about your experience.

Please do not worry if you do not feel anything – not feeling is feeling. If it feels too intense or like it's giving you the 'ick' this suggests that you need to practice being in your body. I recommend taking 10 breaths with one hand on your heart and one on your navel at the same time daily.

The aim is to make right your relationship with yourself by forgiving yourself – you don't need to know what for. The act itself can facilitate reconciliation and help rebuild connections with aspects of your behavior that have become unconscious. This is a profoundly nourishing demonstration of unconditional love.

//////////////////////////////////////

SELF-COMPASSION

The author Kristen Neff describes self-compassion as being 'warm and understanding toward ourselves when we suffer, fail, or feel inadequate, rather than ignoring our pain or flagellating ourselves with self-criticism.'[3]

From a somatic point of view, when we consider how our bodies feel, compassion kisses us on the forehead. It hugs us until our bodies become flooded with oxytocin and soften. Compassion strokes our hair and says, 'I'm listening. Take your time. I'm here.' Compassion says, 'It doesn't matter what you did or what happened; you deserve tenderness.' Compassion says 'Come here little one; I've got you.'

Compassion might feel more like an attack to begin with because it thaws the icy layers we have developed as protection from all the hurt inflicted by others and ourselves. It's like a healing arrow going to the heart of the matter. Or when the kindness of a stranger makes us cry. I found school incredibly anxiety-inducing. I didn't know that at the time, and – let's face it – we weren't talking about mental health and well-being in the 1980s and 1990s in the way we do now. As such, I didn't know that I was anxious. I just knew that school filled me with a sense of dread. I learned to cope by not feeling. I closed myself off from feeling my emotions and sensations (disassociation) so I could function. This childhood adaptation became a maladaptation in adulthood, which meant I didn't know how I felt. I was always 'fine.' Actually, I was frozen, high-functioning, and numb. It meant that when anyone tried to show me compassion, I'd be repulsed. I confused it with pity, and I certainly did not want that. I was a 'strong Black woman' after all.

In 2016, during my existential crisis, I was too fragile to be strong, so during my first coaching session with my first-ever coach Nicola Rae, founder of A Life More Inspired, I was able to receive compassion for the first time. I was being really hard on myself and talking about my procrastinating as if I was choosing to be lazy and leave things to the last minute. Nicola shared that this sounded more like limiting beliefs than laziness. I felt the words in the pit of my stomach. Instantly, I was taken back to how I was at school and in my career. I realized that I had been running on a 'dreadmill' (yes, dreadmill) trying to escape internalized shame and blame. This led me to try and overcompensate for my perceived flaws by working too much. I was constantly trying to make up for my shortcomings because it was obvious that my potential was so much more attractive than the real me.

Points to Consider

Do you live in that unfulfilling land of always trying to live up to 'your potential' rather than embracing where you are right now?

Compassion says, 'I'll hold your hand while the ice melts and reveals what's been frozen.' It says, 'I'll hold you while you metabolize all you've been holding.' And this can be overwhelming when we have been conditioned to be neutral, convenient. To not get in the way and, above all else, to be productive.

Take it slow, but let the thaw begin.

///

Meeting the real you is not an exercise in navel-gazing. Meeting the real you enables you to meet yourself where you are and expands your capacity for life as it is. Meeting the real you and accepting what you find builds self-trust which, in turn, supports an embodied sense of safety. This builds your emotional capacity to experience reality and people as they are, rather than project who you want them to be. We are social creatures; we thrive in community. When we feel safe and can expand that sense of safety into the wider world, we begin to change not only ourselves but the system itself.

Joy Practice

Embodied Kindness

- Take 10 breaths with one hand on your heart and the other on your navel at the same time daily.

- Breathe in for the count of five, breathe out for the count of five, and imagine your body smiling lovingly with each exhale. Try not to hold your tummy in; allow your breath to fill your belly.

- The aim is to build a kind relationship with yourself. A loving smile is often received as a gesture of kindness.

//

Dear One,

May you always remember the power of pleasure and the importance of honoring your natural rhythms. You are a Divine being, worthy of joy and satisfaction.

Your body is wise and intuitive, guiding you towards wholeness and nourishment. Trust in your wisdom and treat your natural ebbs and flows with reverence.

May you embrace your desires and give yourself permission to indulge in what feels good, for pleasure is a portal to your deepest, most-authentic self.

May you create pleasure within your daily endeavors.

CHAPTER 5

BE NATURALLY PRODUCTIVE

'You were not just born to center your entire existence on work and labor. You were born to heal, to grow, to be of service to yourself and community, to practice, to experiment, to create, to have space, to dream, and to connect.'

Tricia Hersey, *Rest is Resistance*

Productivity is an integral part of our human experience. From the moment we wake up to the time we go to bed, we are engaged in activities that require our productivity. Even as we sleep, we are productive. While we blissfully slumber, our brains eliminate waste, new information is processed, and cells reorganize themselves. Productivity is in our nature. We need to work, create, and produce in order to meet our needs and to fulfill our goals and aspirations. Productivity is part of our self-care. In my work as a coach, I'm passionate about helping my clients create work that supports this. I'm often met with resistance when I introduce this concept as our culture creates an environment where work is the antithesis of self-care. What comes up for you as you think about work being part of your self-care?

We work to earn money that enables us to meet our fundamental human needs as well as our wants and desires: this is self-care. When we remember this, we can also create a life that aligns with our values, passions, and aspirations rather than make productivity the end goal. This is why being a friend to your nervous system and meeting the real you are essential. Without meaningful self-knowledge, you'll fill yourself with the perceptions of others and work will be used to ameliorate the lack of connection you have with your life. With self-knowledge and an understanding of what gives your life meaning your work is no longer at the center – you are, and what you do to create a living becomes part of your life rather than the dominant factor.

Productivity is not just about getting things done; it's about the journey of life. It's about beginnings and endings, creation and stagnation, love and loss. It can be an opportunity for transformation. Our productivity can be a conduit for our imagination, helping us to dream ourselves into new possibilities that once felt impossible. So much of what we experience in life was previously a figment of someone's imagination. In the words of author EbonyJanice Moore, we can 'dream ourselves free.'[1] Working with the power of our imaginations to see the world as we wish to experience it gives us hope and impetus to take action in service of our dreams instead of adapting to what at times feels like a nightmare.

HEALTHY LIFE ETHIC

Many people focus on work ethic rather than life ethic because most of us have been conditioned to believe that we must dedicate our lives to work to achieve success. This is why we struggle to rest, and our lives are dominated by work to a degree that what we do shapes our identity. Consequently, people often feel lost when they are not working. I believe it would be healthier to consider work as contributing to our success and for success to be defined as thriving. Work ethic is the belief in the moral value of hard work and diligence (similar to religion), and it's often considered a virtue that leads to success and prosperity. If this was the case, working-class people would be millionaires. In contrast, *life ethic*, which includes work as one aspect of a person's life, focuses on achieving harmony between work, family, health, and personal interests, which is holistic and centers the person rather than the profession.

A good work ethic is emphasized in the workplace because employers want to recruit and retain employees who are reliable, dedicated, and productive (devoted). Sadly, this is usually at the expense of their lives (forsaking all others). The people who are early to work, last to leave, and constantly taking on additional tasks are lauded by people who pay little or no attention to how this impacts their lives. To this end, a good work ethic overshadows the other aspects of life. For women, who bear most of the childcare responsibilities, this is particularly challenging, and even has a name – 'The Motherhood Penalty.' Henley Business School reports that 'the motherhood penalty impacts on aspects of women's careers such as pay, promotion, and the ability to gain good quality employment.'[2] In 2015 the Equality and Human Rights Commission (EHRC) reported that up to 54,000 women in the UK could be forced to leave their jobs due to pregnancy discrimination.[3] Employers may also reward employees who are able to spend more time at work with promotions, pay increases, and bonuses (blessings). Work has become a religion.

In a world where money equals worth, commodifying yourself for external validation and financial abundance is always short-lived because money and praise cannot satiate a malnourished soul.

Outside of employment, a good work ethic looks like being dedicated to maintaining an Instagram-grid-worthy home and prioritizing the needs of others in exchange for accolades such as being selfless, houseproud, and, of course, the coveted 'good girl' title, which in adulthood becomes the good woman, good wife, good mum, and good friend. For women, this constitutes 'The Second Shift,' where domestic and emotional labor are done after a day's paid work.[4] We have been conditioned to prioritize what we do over who we are. A healthy life ethic promotes harmony between work and other aspects of life. It's about productivity that enables you to live in the center of your life, not just around the edges.

Similarly, patriarchal expectations are based on women suppressing their pleasure and power and giving it to men. This happens in boardrooms where men talk over women and in bedrooms where women's pleasure is often hit and miss, literally. A lack of pleasure can limit our ability to live fully. Instead, our productivity is used to numb ourselves while we appease others, which usually leads to over-functioning. By prioritizing our own well-being and cultivating pleasure and power, we can understand our limits and set boundaries that honor who we are.

Embracing your natural productivity levels is like alchemy – turning your perceived limitations into gold. When you recognize your limits, you can work in partnership with yourself rather than against. Embracing your natural productivity enables you to leverage your strengths, honor your limits, and seek aligned support. Perceived weakness is transformed into something you have not been designed to do – just as wisteria doesn't bloom in autumn and snow doesn't fall in summer. Intentionally designed by nature to be as they are rather than conform, wisteria isn't 'wrong' for blooming in spring, snow isn't 'weak' for avoiding summer. You are not weak for not being productive all the time. This is not how we were designed. Understanding your natural productivity gives you the ability to structure your life to bring out the best in you. For example, I'm a terrible administrator. Until I could afford an assistant, I used technology to do as many administrative tasks as possible.

Reimagine Your Ideal, Well-Balanced Day

Reflect on Your Priorities

List your top three time-consuming activities from the previous week.

Next to each activity, rate its fulfillment level on a scale of 1–5 (1 being not fulfilling at all, 5 being extremely fulfilling).

Visualize Balance

Quickly write down what a well-balanced day looks like for you. Don't overthink this or judge yourself – this is an exercise to provide you with information to support transformation. Think about it being a day where you intentionally create time for work, personal time, relationships, and self-care.

Your Life Ethic Statement

Based on your visualization, create a short statement about what constitutes a well-balanced day. For example: *A well-balanced day begins with a good night's sleep, one and a half hours of personal time spread throughout the day and starting with 15 minutes to myself at the start and end of the day. Five hours of productive work, three hours with family/partner.* Remember, this is an *ideal* day, so it doesn't matter if it doesn't feel realistic. This is about partnering with your imagination to support transformation.

One Step Forward

Identify *one* change you can make this week to move closer to your vision of your ideal well-balanced day. Aim for something you can implement easily, for example waking up 15 minutes earlier to have that time to yourself before your day begins.

Affirmation

Write a short affirmation, such as *I have the power to dedicate time to my well-being.* Then put it somewhere you'll see it often. My suggestion is to have it somewhere that is in view as soon as you wake up. For some extra spice, you can set alarms on your smartphone and use the affirmation as the label for the alarm, so when they go off the affirmation appears on your screen. When I was at my lowest, I had affirmation reminders set to go off six times a day. I needed each of those reminders!

Habit Stack

Once you develop your first habit, you can add another. Based on the example above, it could be implementing a bedtime routine 15 minutes before you go to bed or setting aside time to plan your work schedule.

I recommend revisiting this exercise every three months, as this gives you enough time to implement your new habit and track your progress.

//

Although this work begins at an individual level, we must not view it as an individual issue to solve. The system of capitalism emphasizes individualism, which can manifest as us holding ourselves responsible for systemic issues. For example, blaming ourselves for poor time management when we are already over our capacity is not an individual issue. It's a product of a culture where everything is deemed to be urgent, with no care for the human who has to carry out the task. These expectations are mechanical when we are cyclical. It's essential that we recognize that capitalism is a broad social, political, and economic system that permeates our entire existence and informs our individual decisions.

In countries such as the UK and USA, dedicating your life to work is not only seen as respectable – it's honorable, and used as a measure of your worth, whereas in countries such as Italy and Denmark, leisure time and work–life balance are more of a priority. According to the Organization for Economic Cooperation and Development (OECD), the average working week in Denmark has been between 32.7 and 33.7 hours a week since 2010.[5] This provides more time to prioritize the things that contribute to feeling alive, such as family, friends, and personal pursuits. Furthermore, the World Economic Forum (WEF) reports that childcare costs in Denmark are capped, which makes childcare for working parents more accessible.[6] This provides relief for women who do the majority of childcare.

The emphasis on gender equality within the Danish labor market means that women are being employed at higher rates and reducing the gender employment and pay gaps, which are among the lowest among the OECD nations. These policies create a greater sense of fulfillment among the Danish people, both in their personal and professional lives. Rather than toxic levels of work-based productivity, they are more able to live productive lives which include their work.

Their policies and practices uphold the principle of social care; consequently, they have created a society that values and supports families with young children. Their public spending on family benefits is a testament to this, with over 4 percent of GDP dedicated to family services including childcare. This is compared to the OECD average of only 2.6 percent.[7]

This investment reflects their commitment to nurturing the well-being and flourishing of their citizens – citizens, not commodities to be extracted from.

THE DANCE OF CAPITALISM VS THE RHYTHM OF NATURE

If life were a dance floor, capitalism would be dancing to the words instead of the beat, while nature vibes to the rhythm.

Capitalism prioritizes profit over people and planet. This can be compared to dancing to the lyrics of a song rather than the beat, which is the essence of the music. Nature operates in a rhythm that is consistent and harmonious. Nature is a dancer who moves to the rhythm of the music, with a deep sense of connection and alignment with the surrounding environment.

If we can collectively remember how to dance to the rhythm of nature, rather than just the lyrics of capitalism, we can achieve a more sustainable and harmonious (pun intended) future. This means rebuilding economic systems, so they prioritize social and environmental responsibility, and working to protect the natural resources that support life on Earth. There are already examples of this in practice. In the USA, the Stewart's Shops convenience store chain operates under the ESOP (Employee Stock Ownership Plan) model. Under this model, employees can own shares in the company if they meet the requirements. Consequently, over 170 Stewart's employees own over 40 percent of the company.

While capitalism has facilitated many technological advancements and created economic growth, it's important to remember that nature provides the fundamental resources and systems that sustain all life on this planet. We need to redress the imbalance between the pursuit of economic growth and our responsibility to protect and preserve our natural environment, including the first natural environment we inhabit: our bodies.

CAPITALISM PRIORITIZES
PROFIT OVER PEOPLE
AND PLANET. THIS CAN BE
COMPARED TO DANCING TO
THE LYRICS OF A SONG RATHER
THAN THE BEAT, WHICH IS THE
ESSENCE OF THE MUSIC.

HORMONAL CYCLES

A more balanced approach in relation to our nature and the natural world would support the cyclical nature of productivity. This could have significant benefits for women and people who menstruate and our natural cycles. Women and menstruating people's bodies operate within an intricate hormonal system that regulates various biological, emotional, and psychological functions. This includes menstrual cycles, pregnancy, childbirth, perimenopause, and menopause, which are all influenced by environmental and social factors.

For menstruating women and people who menstruate, the menstrual cycle usually consists of four hormonal phases: the menstrual phase, follicular phase, ovulatory phase, and luteal phase.

Here's a brief overview of each phase:

• **Menstrual phase:** This is the beginning of the cycle. It starts on the first day of bleeding and generally lasts for three to seven days. Levels of the hormones estrogen and progesterone are at their lowest and it is hard to ignore what is happening and how you're feeling during this phase as there is physical evidence via the menstrual bleed.

• **Follicular phase:** This begins on day one of menstruation and lasts approximately two weeks. Follicles gradually develop on the ovaries and one of them will become dominant and release a mature egg. During the second week of this phase, hormones such as estrogen begin to rise, preparing the body for ovulation.

• **Ovulatory phase:** This is when the mature egg is released by the follicle. This part of the cycle lasts between three and five days. Estrogen and luteinizing hormones are at their highest during this phase.

- **Luteal phase:** This begins after ovulation. The unfertilized egg becomes *corpus luteum*, which tells your body you're not pregnant and phase one repeats unless you're pregnant. This phase lasts approximately 10 to 14 days.

From puberty to menopause, our bodies do this every single month. Even if you knew this already, I invite you to pause for a moment and take in how wondrous your body is. Your biology is miraculous!

Working too much can negatively impact women during any of these phases; for example:

- **Menstrual phase:** Women may experience fatigue, cramps, and mood swings. Working long hours or excessive stress can exacerbate these symptoms. Additionally, the stress hormone cortisol can lead to light or delayed periods. Depending on the way your body manages stress, periods can stop altogether. This is called amenorrhea, which is when stress prevents your brain from sending the correct signals to your hormones. Due to our conditioning, we will take medication, natural remedies, and try all the 'hacks' to suppress our symptoms and carry on as usual – aka as men do – to the detriment of our health. Medication and hacks address the symptoms; we need to address the cause. Life includes stress. A certain amount of stress is healthy, but the pattern of working too much the way we do is not just unhealthy. It suppresses our humanity and dismisses our natural intelligence, damaging our relationship with ourselves. Instead of tending to our pain, we try to shut it up by telling ourselves to 'be brave.' Does that sound familiar?

- **Follicular phase:** The beginning of this phase (menstruation) can make us prone to mood changes, lack of focus, and fatigue because your body is working hard and requires more rest. Working too much during this phase is literally working against your nature. While it is unrealistic to down tools for a week each month, it is necessary to prioritize self-care – including naps if possible, going for walks, gentle yoga, eating nourishing foods, and good sleep and sleep hygiene.

- **Ovulatory phase:** Although this is the 'summer' of our cycle, where we usually experience increased energy and zest for life, some women experience breast tenderness and bloating. Due to the increased energy, it's easy to push too hard during this phase. This is not advisable. As we learned in junior school maths, what's borrowed must be carried! Going too hard during this phase will impact phase four. Where you can go hard, though, is with your intentional physical movement, such as increasing or slowing down your reps for more intensity during strength training, dynamic yoga, hiking, or the big DIY project you've wanted to get done.

- **Luteal phase:** Due to hormonal shifts that are preparing to nurture an embryo or shed uterine lining, mood changes are more likely, as are anxiety and fatigue. Our life-force energy is devoted to the business of life creation or preparing to clear cells and lining that won't be needed. When our bodies are working so hard for the possibility of growing an embryo and birthing a child, there is no time for stress and working too much. When a pregnancy has not been conceived progesterone levels fall, making us more prone to exhaustion. We literally have two vibrant weeks per month – half a year!

In our modern, patriarchal world, women face numerous challenges in navigating work, family, relationships, and personal responsibilities. For women and people who menstruate, this balance can be even more challenging, as their hormonal cycles can impact physical and emotional well-being.

I know that this looks like doom and gloom, but by understanding your menstrual cycles and learning how to take care of yourself, you can find a path to healthy productivity and well-being. The menstrual cycle is complex and a vital sign of health that requires more intentional care than viewing it as an inconvenience and suppressing it with medicine. Since we have begun to talk about periods and menstrual health publicly, we have been able to reduce the stigma and advocate for ourselves.

When I was at school, being on your period was like a CIA assignment. We would go to great lengths to hide sanitary pads and tampons up our sleeves. We'd sit in toilet cubicles trying to rip our sanitary pads off their envelopes at the speed of light or as slow as a sloth in an attempt to conceal the fact that a very normal healthy monthly event was taking place. Now my teenage daughter tells me that she and her friends 'proudly' hold their sanitary products as they go to the toilet. I have also overheard her and her friends on group video calls with male friends talking about being hormonal and the boys responding with empathy or a joke to make them laugh.

> *'If we can share our story with someone*
> *who responds with empathy and*
> *understanding, shame can't survive.'*
> **Brené Brown**

The application of knowledge is power. By tracking your menstrual cycle and paying attention to your hormonal phases, you can develop a better understanding of your needs throughout the month. This knowledge can help you plan your schedule and workload more effectively, leading to improved productivity and well-being.

For example, I don't believe my doubts from days 22–28 of my cycle, as my inner critic is very strong, mean, and loud due to PMS. During this phase of my cycle, as far as I'm concerned, I'm the worst, and I can recall mistakes from 1989, 1997, and 2003 as if they occurred yesterday. I'm also irritable AF. I recognize this, as my 'tells' are a lack of patience, which manifests as tutting all the time and rage if I have to explain myself more than once. When I feel irritated, I can stop myself and remind myself that it's probably my hormones being an asshole. This prevents me from shaming myself and reminds me that I need extra tenderness.

Where possible, I try to schedule work that requires a high level of energy from day six to 16 of my cycle as during this phase I feel like Grace Jones, Clair Huxtable, Destiny's Child (including the original line up), and Cheetarah (Thunder, Thunder, Thundercats Hoooo). If you come to anything I'm hosting while I'm ovulating, I'm like a rapturous, charismatic cult leader, but in my cult, everyone feels loved and safe enough to be who they are.

I'm by no means suggesting that you only function during the end of your follicular phase and ovulation, but with this information you can preempt your needs and plan accordingly. For example, I always make sure I don't skip my magnesium supplements in the few days before or during my period or I'll live on a diet of Picnic chocolate bars and Thai sweet chili crisps.

A self-care routine that is tailored to your changing needs can help you to manage stressors better and be more alert to the ventral glimmers in life we often overlook. In addition to improved self-care, understanding your menstrual cycle can also lead to better communication with colleagues, friends, and family. By communicating your needs more clearly, you can set boundaries around your schedule and workload, leading to improved relationships and less stress. Some workplaces have responded to the information about the impact of the menstrual cycle by granting menstrual leave. My self-employed clients grant themselves naps and slower days instead of shaming themselves about being weak or lazy.

Cycle Tracking Exercise

For this exercise, I would like you to keep track of your mood, energy, ANS state, and your inner dialogue during your menstrual cycle, paying particular attention to the luteal phase. We tend to judge ourselves based on who we are our best, which means we hold ourselves to standards that are not an accurate reflection of who we are and how we are most of the time. This leads us to shaming ourselves for not always being our best.

Let's look at the meaning of the word 'best.' It means 'of the highest quality, excellence, or standing' or 'most advantageous, suitable, or desirable.'[8] For many of us, this is not sustainable day in day out. Measuring who you are day to day provides more honest data and enables you to make plans and set goals that are SMART (specific, measurable, achievable, realistic, and timely). In terms of the menstrual cycle, it is not uncommon for women to feel like they have superhuman strength during the ovulation phase, but this is a few days of our cycle. Learning who you are during your luteal phase also supports your ovulatory phase.

Keeping track will help you to identify how you shift through different autonomic states throughout your cycle. This will help you understand how your biology impacts your psychology.

Here is an example:

Cycle day	State	Early AM	Late AM	Early PM	Late PM	Early evening	Before bed
25	Mood	Anxious	Calm	Feeling guilty	Apathetic	Irritated	Anxious
	Energy	Low	Medium	Low	Low	Medium	Low
	Inner dialogue	Running out of time	Encouraging	Critical	Critical	Shaming	Strategizing my comeback
	ANS state	Sympathetic	Ventral	Dorsal	Dorsal	Sympathetic	Sympathetic
26	Mood	Overwhelm	Numb	Ashamed	Apathetic	Irritated	Sad
	Energy	Low	Medium	Low	Low	Low	Low
	Inner dialogue	I'm useless	Defeatist	Critical	Critical	Judgmental	I'm not built for this
	ANS state	Dorsal	Dorsal	Dorsal	Dorsal	Dorsal	Dorsal

Tracking my cycle in this way helped me to see that I'm usually dorsal in the late afternoon regardless of the time of the month. This awareness means that I can support myself adequately and where possible schedule my work accordingly. During my luteal phase this looks like doing work that requires focus in the morning, when I have more energy, and doing client-facing work in the afternoon, as the thrill of working with other people activates my sympathetic nervous system, so I have the energy necessary to be present and attuned.

Prior to tracking my cycle and autonomic states in this way I would be my worst critic. With the knowledge I have now, I remind myself it's not me, it's my hormones, and that is enough to turn the inner judgment down.

To get accurate information about your cycle, energy, and ANS states, I suggest tracking for three months. This data can help you understand yourself better and inform your plans.

//

CIRCADIAN RHYTHMS

The regulation of our sleep-wake cycle is managed by our circadian rhythm; it impacts a number of our biological and behavioral processes. For women and birthing people, pregnancy, perimenopause, menopause, and excessive work schedules can be particularly challenging.

According to research by the multidisciplinary scientific journal, *Proceedings of the National Academy of Sciences* (PNAS), the circadian rhythm affects melatonin (sleep hormone) and body temperature.[9] This impacts women's body clocks by making them run an hour earlier than men's, even when the women and men maintain nearly identical sleep and wake times. It also found that generally women wake up earlier than men and tend to prefer morning activities.[10] By aligning our daily routines with our circadian rhythms, we can support healthy productivity and work-life harmony. Here are some suggestions:

• Getting sufficient restful sleep is crucial to maintain a healthy circadian rhythm. While everyone is unique, generally speaking it is advisable for women to aim for seven to eight hours of sleep each night and establish a consistent sleep routine. I'm at my best when I set myself up for eight hours of sleep – however, this is not always successful as I'm perimenopausal and tend to have broken sleep in my luteal phase.

- Create a good sleep routine. We have a tendency to heap ourselves into bed at the end of the day, bringing all the content of the day with us. You will notice parents talking about their children's bedtime routine and how important it is. Well, it doesn't stop being important when we turn 13. A night routine doesn't have to be a whole performance – the simpler the better.

- Start by trying not to be on your phone, tablet, or laptop an hour before bed. In the evening, try to use lower, softer lighting rather than bright/harsh light. Do something to mark the end of the day, such as cleansing your face and brushing your teeth. I recommend using a particular face wash and moisturizer so that you associate the texture and smell with going to bed. When you get into bed, do some progressive muscle relaxation to let go of any tension built up throughout the day. Write down three things you're grateful for from the day and three things you're looking forward to tomorrow. They don't need to be grandiose things. You could be grateful for remembering to stay hydrated or seeing some particularly spectacular cumulonimbus clouds. And you could look forward to your morning coffee or taking your nephew swimming (one of my personal faves).

My nighttime routine begins when I finish my workday. As I work from home, I have to make the effort to 'commute' from work to home. My commute includes reviewing my daily plan, spraying a particular room spray, and ringing my singing bowl. This helps me leave my work at my desk instead of psychologically carrying it with me.

Light exposure plays a significant role in regulating our circadian rhythm. We need to be mindful about our exposure to light throughout the day, especially as we spend so much time indoors. We can do this by seeking natural light during the day and avoiding bright screens or blue light in the evenings.

In the summer months, I sleep with my curtains open so that I'm woken by the sunlight in the mornings. During the winter months, I use a sunlight alarm so that I'm gently woken by light rather than the startling sound of an alarm. This means I have no need for my phone in my bedroom. If my phone is on my bedside table, I'll be on it first thing in the morning acting like the world will stop if I don't check my emails, social media, and WhatsApp before my eyes have adjusted to the light – remember recovery is forever.

Timing exercise appropriately can also support a healthy circadian rhythm. Morning exercise can regulate the sleep-wake cycle and improve productivity, while evening exercise can disrupt sleep. I know that exercising first thing in the morning doesn't work for me. Recovery is longer and I'm tired all day. Exercise between 9 and 11 a.m. is my sweet spot. However, it took me six years to believe this. Instead, I lambasted myself for being 'lazy' because I was trying to force myself into a rhythm that disrupts my natural one!

Building in rest breaks is vital to maintain productivity and prevent burnout, and I include how to create your own rest practice in the next chapter. The circadian rhythm follows a natural cycle of activity and rest, and respecting this cycle can lead to optimal physical and mental health. I always tell my clients that the rest is just as important as the race.

You'll notice that none of these are groundbreaking. This is because the simple things we do every day have a compounding effect. We find this very hard because it is not as exciting as the trends and fads that come and go. But these practices support a healthy foundation that can withstand the challenges of life because they tell your body you're not in survival mode. Meeting these foundational needs builds trust. Your body knows that you'll meet your needs and rewards this trust with more vitality for life.

Understanding our rhythms and supporting them enables productivity that is nourishing, as it enriches the quality of life rather than commodifying the human body and extracting your life force in exchange for profit and external validation.

This is very challenging because we are caught in a vacuum of celebrating how exhausted we are, teetering on the brink of burnout, overworking to produce results (for someone else's gain), while feeling unable to proudly share our accomplishments through fear that we will be judged as uncouth, attention-seeking showoffs. However, if more of us learn and apply the knowledge that we hold in our bodies, we can be the change we want to see. In the words of Marianne Williamson, 'as we let our own light shine, we unconsciously give other people permission to do the same. As we are liberated from our own fear, our presence automatically liberates others.'[11]

Joy practice

Host a gratitude circle. Gather your friends in person or via Zoom and invite them to share what they are grateful for. There are a few rules:

- No giving advice, suggestions, or fixing people. Let their gratitude be theirs and celebrate with them.

- It is a circle focused on gratitude; anything other than this can wait until after the circle.

- If someone doesn't want to share, don't try to encourage them to do so. Trust and respect their choice.

- What is said in the circle stays in the circle.

- It might be helpful to allocate time per person to ensure everyone has time to share. Leave time at the end to say thank you and close the circle. I suggest having a quote, poem, or a passage from a book to read at the end.

///

Dear One,

Embrace the measure of your bandwidth,
for within its sacred boundaries resides
a wellspring of personal power.

Honor the ebbing and flowing of your dynamic
energy as a reflection of the cycles of nature.

Appreciate the delicate dance between the
doing of the things, the making use of your
time, and the whispers of your soul's longing
to be, to breathe easy, to shed and renew.

In this honoring, you unlock a profound path to
self-discovery, authenticity, and connection.

Bless yourself with autonomy to discern,
to say no or not now, and to prioritize
what truly resonates with your spirit.

By embracing your unique bandwidth, you open
the gateway to a life that feels like your own.

With daily glimmers of satisfaction, joy,
purpose, and happiness that compound
together, weaving a tapestry of fulfillment.

Take in the good, savor it, drink it in, let it fill your
body like a wicked bassline, and delight as your world
transforms into a symphony of harmonious living.

CHAPTER 6

KNOW YOUR BANDWIDTH

'Your no makes the way for your yes.

Boundaries create the container within which your yes is authentic.

Being able to say no makes yes a choice.'

Adrienne Maree Brown

Your body is your personal land, your sovereign state. Your skin – your biggest organ – is your highly sophisticated boundary, where thousands of nerve endings connect with the outside world using the skill of neuroception to detect signs of safety and danger below the level of your conscious mind. Feeding back data that tells you when to stop, go, and when to say yes, no, or let's see. A feedback loop reminding you of what and who you need to be in times of uncertainty. Your body is your own intelligent counsel.

Your body is a beautifully sophisticated sensory system that's constantly alerting you to your bandwidth. Through your felt sense, autonomic reactions, goosebumps, twinges, and pleasurable sensations, it's providing you with guidance about what feels good and what doesn't.

When you treat yourself like the sovereign being you are, you'll treat the land like it's sovereign because you'll recognize the land as home. No more exploiting yourself beyond your capacity, commodifying yourself for material gain and external validation with a short shelf life. No more exploiting the land beyond its capacity, no more commodifying the soil, hoarding its wealth, and allowing the excess to decay in landfill. As a sovereign being, you'll recognize the signals from your body as a bid for connection or a request for care, and collectively we will recognize signals from the land in the same way. No more wasting time debating and negotiating the terms.

Our relationship with the land has become distant because machines have taken over the work that was once done with our hands, severing our connection to what sustains us. In turn, we have become distant from ourselves as we lose connection to ourselves while coveting and copying the speed and efficiency of said machinery. But we are not mechanical, we are cyclical, waxing and waning like the moon, each phase as vital as the next. Our culture makes it challenging to remember that all our phases are important, as so much emphasis is placed on shining brightly all the time. Consequently, we overlook signs telling us when it's time to wane into darkness so we can rest and renew. Instead, we resist and try to continue shining brightly, even though it's time to dim the lights for a while.

To move through life as you know it, you have to become disconnected from your body. It's the only way you can perfect the coping mechanism of ignoring the signals it's sending so you can push yourself beyond your limits and dismiss the wisdom you've amassed since the dawn of creation. We call this a 'can-do' attitude and a positive mindset. It's a sweet nectar for capitalism.

Our culture woefully fails to recognize the validity of women's bodily experiences. We're conditioned to subdue and deny communication from our bodies, suppressing our natural instincts and wisdom for the sake of being squeezed into societal expectations. This enables us to engage in the inhumane timescales of urgency culture where we are rewarded with saccharine praise and 'just enough' to exist.

But it doesn't have to be this way. As women, we have the power to reclaim our bodies and embrace the wisdom they offer. It starts with listening to the signals they're sending and honoring our limits and boundaries.

It's all too easy to look at a woman with financial success, desirable material goods, and qualifications and accolades and assume that she has it all together. Society often equates success with material possessions and outward appearances, but the truth is that our bodies don't care about any of that. Nervous systems don't co-regulate with Hermès.

Our bodies are not impressed by degrees, new clients, or designer bags. They don't care about job titles, bank accounts, or social media followings. What they do care about is being heard and respected. When your body is heard and respected, you are heard and respected.

The pressure to maintain a certain image can often exacerbate the separation of mind from body. Women who are constantly under the scrutiny of society may feel the need to suppress their bodies' signals in order to maintain a convenient facade.

But this only perpetuates the cycle of disconnection and disregard for our bodies' wisdom. It's vital that we learn how to be in right relationship with ourselves and treat our bodies with reverence because we are holy, all-powerful, all-mighty. And in a system that relies on us being scattered and shattered, learning to honor your bandwidth is an act of resistance.

Exercise

For the purpose of this chapter, I invite you to consider your bandwidth/capacity as the basis for your boundaries. I'll use bandwidth and capacity interchangeably.

You can do this exercise standing or sitting, but please do not engage in this activity if you're driving or operating heavy machinery.

- I invite you to sit or stand still and look straight ahead as you normally would. Then very gently turn your head to the right as far as you can go without straining. The moment you can feel any tension whatsoever I want you to stop and bring your head back to center. Now do the same thing, turning your head toward the left. As soon as you feel any tension at all, stop and bring your head back to center.

- Next, tilt your head forward, going down toward your chest as far as you can go without any strain. The moment you feel pulling or tension, stop and lift your head back to center. And now tilt your head backward, as far as you can – again without any strain or pulling.

- Now do the same movements and allow yourself to turn and tilt your head as far as you can stretch without hurting yourself. Take a moment to notice the difference between the range of movement without strain and the range when you stretch.

The 'movement without strain' is the natural boundary of your neck. The stretched movement goes beyond your natural boundary. Bearing this in mind:

- What sensations did you experience when you reached your natural boundary while turning and tilting your head? How would you describe the feeling?

- Reflecting on your experience, what do you think your neck's natural boundary represents in terms of your natural boundaries?

- How does becoming aware of your natural boundaries provide valuable data or information about the difference between your capacity and capability?

- Did you feel a sense of connection or disconnect with your body while performing the exercise? If so, can you describe that experience and what it might indicate about your day-to-day connection with your body?

- In what ways can understanding your natural boundaries enhance your overall well-being and empower you to be mindful of your capacity and capability, reducing overwhelm and burnout?

///

I shared this exercise so you can experience first-hand the distinction between your natural boundaries and the strain we often impose on ourselves by constantly pushing beyond them. While it's true that some people may possess greater flexibility, and that with dedicated practice, over time, we can all expand our range of movement, this exercise provides you with a tangible understanding of the disparity between your capacity and capability. It's a reminder that we frequently find ourselves with our necks turned excessively in one direction or the other, perpetually overextending ourselves in pursuit of productivity and speed. While there may be practical reasons to occasionally exceed our natural range of movement, it's crucial to acknowledge that this is not our innate state of being.

Constantly living in a state of pushing beyond our natural boundaries can have negative consequences for our well-being. Overextending ourselves without awareness or boundaries takes a toll on our mental and emotional health, contributing to feelings of overwhelm, burnout, and decreased overall resilience. Ignoring our natural limits may prevent us from fully connecting with our bodies and recognizing the signs of exhaustion or stress. Ultimately, failing to respect our natural boundaries can disrupt the delicate harmony between our capacity and capability, disrupting our relationships with ourselves, hindering our ability to connect with others, and creating an existence rather than a life.

> *'Tell me, what is it you plan to do with*
> *your one wild and precious life?'*
> **Mary Oliver, 'The Summer Day'**
> **from *House of Light***

My former client and friend Vickie Remoe, CEO and founder of VR&C Marketing, joined our group-coaching Zoom call looking unlike herself. Vickie is a trailblazing, culture-shifting West African woman and marketing expert. She has clients all over Africa and the USA. She is a regular guest on *BBC Africa*, shining brightly contributing to topical discussions, sharing her opinions and expertise. She is luminescent like the full moon, her eyes sparkle like stars, her skin glows like the sea at night, not just because of her rich melanin and exposure to the African sunshine. Her glow comes from within.

This woman is magnetic and naturally stands out in a crowd but on this day, instead of Vickie being multidimensional, she seemed flat.

As she began to share how she was and what she was experiencing, I could smell the familiar scent of smoking embers. I asked her if this could be burnout. Vickie has a lot of responsibility. It was the pandemic; her business was on an enforced pause, and she was paying her staff's salaries from her personal income, as she was acutely aware of how not being paid would impact her staff team in her Sierra Leone office. With no furlough or welfare system, her staff would not be able to meet their essential needs. The knowledge of this and trying to keep a business afloat during the biggest health emergency of our times was naturally putting Vickie under immense strain.

However, Vickie is used to working according to her capability rather than her capacity. She is well-educated and determined with a strong purpose. She is a change-maker; her work is values-driven, and she is here to make a difference. This means that she has learned how to override her capacity with a focused mindset so that she can fulfill her purpose and responsibilities. This is what we are primed for from reception class through to higher education. We are taught to keep going.

Vickie contemplated my question about burnout, then responded that it was not burnout – she was merely 'tired.' This is not uncommon. When faced with our limitations, we often go into denial because we are hooked on who we think we should be instead of being present with who we are.

Rather than going through the phases of grief (denial, anger, depression, bargaining, acceptance)[1] as we transition through the phases of life, leaving former parts of ourselves behind, we go into survival mode, fighting against the inevitable, spending too long in denial, busying ourselves to avoid emotions that highlight what we need and how delicate we are. Below the surface of busyness, abandonment and pushing through, feelings asking us to change become feelings of anxiety and depression, culminating in burnout and/or mental ill health.

'When our grief cannot be spoken, it falls into the
shadow and re-arises in us as symptoms. So many of
us are depressed, anxious, and lonely. We struggle with
addictions and find ourselves moving at a breathless
pace, trying to keep up with the machinery of culture.'
Francis Weller, *The Wild Edge of Sorrow*

Due to our conditioning, we tend to override overwhelm, helplessness, grief, and fear with denial and busyness, frittering away our life force by bouncing up and down the autonomic ladder instead of enduring the temporary pain of processing our feelings.

The following week Vickie returned to our group, realizing that she was indeed burned out. Her anxiety about the well-being of her staff was real and called for and it was also a mask for deeper unprocessed emotions, which manifested as selflessness and had led to depletion.

Our conditioning tells us that this type of selflessness is virtuous, but I invite you to look at the word 'selfless.' Say the word slowly: selfless. Self-less. Put your hand on your navel and say the word slowly again, self-less. How does the notion of being 'selfless' feel in your body? And remember, if you feel numb that means you're feeling something. It is likely that your numbness is protecting you from feeling what you have learned to suppress. Whether you feel something or feel nothing, I invite you to carry this question with you today and see what comes up. There is no pass or fail – it's an experiment.

When I feel into selflessness, I experience sensations that feel like churning fog in my abdomen and a slight shallowing of my breath. I have a vision of me being engulfed by fog. Life goes on around me while I'm barely visible. People keep bumping into me because they can hardly see me, and although they are the ones bumping into me, I smile and apologize repeatedly. This does not feel powerful or kind. The people who bump into me can't see that they are creating new bruises on top of old ones. They don't realize I'm injured and weak because they see me smiling and apologizing to them for hurting me. This does not feel empowered, or generous. This denial of self feels depleting, abusive, and corrosive. Invariably, these feelings get projected onto others in the form of bitter indignation – no fun for anyone.

Vickie's burnout was a reflection of the emptiness inside as she took what was hers to give to others. Although this was and is a nice gesture, the cost was too high and the long-term impact too deep. We explored strategies that would enable Vickie to support her staff without depleting herself so that her needs could be met, too.

Knowing your boundaries is essential.

- Do you often feel overwhelmed by the demands of your work or personal life?

- Are you struggling to meet deadlines, manage your time, or achieve your goals?

- Are you often tired regardless of how much sleep you get?

- Do you often feel put upon, like things won't happen unless you do them?

- Do you do things because you think it is expected or because you'll feel bad if you don't?

If so, you may benefit from understanding your boundaries. Knowing your limits and setting clear boundaries can help you work more efficiently, prioritize your tasks, and achieve greater success in all areas of your life.

> *'Boundaries are the distance at which I can*
> *love you and me simultaneously.'*
> **Prentice Hemphill**

WHAT ARE BOUNDARIES?

UC Berkeley describes boundaries as, 'the limits and rules we set for ourselves within relationships.'[2] They are the 'rules' we create for ourselves in terms of our time, energy, and resources. They define what we are willing and able to do, and what we can't or shouldn't do. Boundaries can be physical, emotional, or psychological, and they can change over time.

Having boundaries is challenging for most of us, regardless of gender. And children's boundaries are often ignored and at times considered to be rude. For example, being forced to cuddle people they don't want to, being forced to smile and 'look nice' for photos they don't want to be in, being told that taking GCSE art is a waste and being persuaded to study something deemed more academic instead. Our intuitive knowing is denied and replaced with the performance of being polite, nice, or practical for the benefit of people/systems of dominant power. This lays the foundation of a psychological contract that will become a hindrance in later life.

Knowing what your boundaries need to be gives you the power to enter healthy relationships and advocate for yourself rather than people-please. People often consider boundaries as a barrier.

KNOWING WHAT YOUR BOUNDARIES NEED TO BE GIVES YOU THE POWER TO ENTER HEALTHY RELATIONSHIPS AND ADVOCATE FOR YOURSELF RATHER THAN PEOPLE-PLEASE.

However, they support honesty and genuine relationships that are spacious and safe enough for you to be whole.

The Benefits of Knowing Your Boundaries

Knowing your boundaries can have numerous benefits, including:

- Understanding your boundaries enables you to prioritize your tasks and responsibilities effectively, which means you'll spend less time proving yourself and more time on the work that matters. This will help you to distinguish between what is important, what requires immediate attention, and what can wait. This allows you to make the best use of your time and energy.

- Understanding your boundaries helps you manage your time more effectively. Women give their time so freely without considering the wider impact. Instead, we believe that we are inefficient. It is not uncommon for my clients to refer to themselves as lazy or unorganized when actually, their lack of boundaries means they are not planning their time, while also trying to do everything they have on their plate simultaneously. Their days are full, but they have no direction. Consequently, each day feels like the TV program *Total Wipeout* – but with no winners. Allocating time to specific tasks or activities can reduce time spent on them as you have to focus. It allows you to see how long things *actually* take so you can be realistic in the time you allocate. This also helps you see where you need support.

- Knowing what your boundaries are helps you make aligned decisions, from the division of labor to work tasks and whether or not you should join the PTA – do not join the PTA! Your boundaries are very closely linked to your values; upholding your boundaries keeps you in integrity, enabling you to make powerful decisions even when they don't feel 'nice.' It helps reduce over-committing and spreading yourself too thin, which leads to exhaustion, resentment, and frustration, which can reduce productivity.

- Knowing your boundaries requires self-awareness and acceptance. It means being aware of your needs, strengths, and limitations and not making yourself wrong for them. This self-awareness can help you identify areas where you need to grow, be supported, or delegate tasks to others. By acknowledging your boundaries, you can avoid taking on tasks that will take you over your bandwidth. This may sound limiting, but it is the difference between constantly accelerating, speeding, and overtaking only to be joined by the car you overtook at the traffic lights.

How to Set Boundaries

Setting boundaries can be challenging. It can feel uncomfortable and at times could trigger signs of danger because it may mean saying 'no' or 'not now' to people you value or people with power. There are strategies you can use to make setting boundaries easier:

- **Have clear values:** Values are beliefs that help us identify what is 'good' or 'bad', and what is most important. Your values will guide you in setting boundaries that align with your goals and priorities.

- **Be specific:** Specificity allows us to understand what our values mean to us so we can clearly communicate them to others.

If you're unclear about your boundaries, other people will be unclear too and this lack of clarity will lead to confusion.

- **Practice self-care:** Taking care of yourself physically, emotionally, and mentally helps support regulation and healthy choices. It's hard to have effective boundaries when you're dysregulated and in survival mode.

- **Learn to say no:** Saying no can be terrifying, but it is essential to set boundaries. It's possible to learn to say no politely and respectfully, and offer alternatives where possible. For example, when your boss asks you to take on additional work you could say, 'I'm unable to take on this task in addition to my current workload as it will negatively impact the quality of my work. I'll have more capacity at the end of next week.' Or to be clear about your intentions; for example, 'I love that you want to invite friends round for dinner. This week is very busy, so I'd like a quiet weekend. How about inviting them next week, instead?'

Feel Your Feelings

Our bodies send us signals all the time. We often miss these signals, as our brains are galloping through time so quickly that we bypass our feelings.

- I invite you to recall three or four 'low-level' times when you said yes when you didn't want to. For example, 'small' things such as agreeing to care for children when you needed time for yourself, taking on extra work when you were already overloaded, or going out when you'd rather have curled up with a book. Remember, gentle is effective! See if you can remember any feelings or sensations just before you said yes, after you said yes, or during the thing you didn't want to do.

- When I did this exercise, I realized that I felt a churning sensation just before I said yes and then a sinking feeling afterward. This is how my body communicates resentment. This exercise showed me how often I felt resentment because of all the yeses I didn't mean. Now I take a moment to check in with myself before saying yes. If I'm uncertain, it's a polite no or not now. There are occasions where I have to say yes but it is a conscious choice rather than default programming.

- If you're unable to identify any sensations next time you're asked to do something, take a moment to see if you feel any sensations.

///

Boundaries may feel difficult in the beginning but over time they can support healthy connection. Also, boundaries are for you to uphold; they are not rules for other people. If you do not want to stay up late stacking the dishwasher, you must honor that. If you want your partner to support you, be honest and tell them that routinely staying up late to stack the dishwasher is creating resentment and you would like to share this task by each of you doing it on alternate days, for example.

REST FOR RESTORATION

In my experience, overriding your capacity in favor of your capability is easy to do in your twenties and early thirties. It's a rite of passage, a gift of youth. But as we reach our mid-thirties, our body skillfully shows us that it's the boss, and all that energy youth allowed us to borrow so freely must be repaid. This is a harsh truth that few people get to escape. The remedy can't be a hack, how-to, or quick fix. It must be radical self-care.

> 'Honoring your own boundaries is the clearest
> message to others to honor them, too.'
>
> **Gina Greenlee, *Postcards and Pearls***

The groundbreaking work of Saundra Dalton-Smith, M.D. offers an integrated framework for healing burnout and reducing the likelihood of its recurrence. Dr. Dalton-Smith's 'seven types of rest'[3] provides a holistic approach to rest. It's not merely the act of doing nothing. She presents different types of rest as a means of nurturing our well-being.

- **Physical rest**, the first type, involves addressing the fatigue that burnout often inflicts on our bodies. It encompasses not only getting sufficient sleep but also engaging in activities that promote relaxation and rejuvenation, such as gentle stretching, massages, or simply allowing ourselves to rest without guilt.

- **Mental rest** is the second type and entails finding respite for our overburdened minds. The incessant chatter of thoughts and the constant mental stimulation of modern life can deplete our cognitive reserves. By consciously engaging in activities that cultivate a sense of peace, such as mindfulness, meditation, or creative pursuits, we support mental restoration.

- **Emotional rest**, the third type, recognizes the emotional toll of burnout. It involves acknowledging and addressing the emotional exhaustion that is common for women in patriarchal society. This type of rest is the hardest, as it is an internal need that can be glossed over with makeup, a power suit, and gritted teeth. It requires courage to seek sensitive support from loved ones or professionals. If you feel unable to ask for help (and even if you're able to), I highly recommend journaling; offloading your emotions onto a page in a private notebook can be cathartic and help you make sense of your experience. When I was at my lowest and feeling too fragile to access therapy, journaling was my savior. Emotional rest also includes activities that bring us joy and comfort. I recommend board games. For extra house points, I recommend inviting friends over to play board games with you.

- **Social rest** is the fourth type. This acknowledges the importance of nurturing, meaningful connections where you feel safe enough to be whole. Burnout often isolates us, leaving us feeling disconnected. Cultivating authentic relationships, engaging in activities with loved ones, and finding community support can help counteract the social deprivation imposed by burnout.

- **Sensory rest**, the fifth type, focuses on finding respite from the sensory overload of our modern world. Constant exposure to noise, screens, and stimuli can overwhelm our senses. Engaging in activities that provide moments of sensory calm, such as spending time in nature, taking soothing baths, breath work, or grounding practices, can provide relief from the hustle and bustle of the world.

- **Creative rest**, the sixth type, recognizes the need to tap into our innate creativity. Burnout can stifle our creative expression, leaving us feeling numb and restless. Exploring hobbies or allowing ourselves the freedom to play and create without judgment can reignite our creative sparks and glimmers of joy.

- **Spiritual rest** is the seventh and final type, which goes beyond religious beliefs and encompasses a sense of purpose and connection to something greater than ourselves. Nurturing our spiritual well-being may involve meditation, prayer, chanting, or spending time in nature. It involves finding meaning and aligning our actions with our deepest values. According to Dr. Emma Seppala, the Science Director of Stanford University's Center for Compassion and Altruism, spiritual people are more likely to engage in stress-reducing activities such as meditation or prayer.[4] She also identifies that spiritual people are more likely to volunteer and benefit from the 'helpers' high,' where people get a profound sense of joy and fulfillment from helping others.

Each type of rest addresses a unique aspect of our being, providing opportunities for restoration and a more sustainable approach to life. In my experience, emotional rest is the key to other types of rest and is usually the most challenging type. Emotional rest requires radical honesty and a level of vulnerability we are not accustomed to in our go-getting society.

One day we will learn that we don't need more coffee to keep us going. We need adequate rest.

Why Rest Is a Practice

Rest can feel hard because we're not used to it and because we are used to doing as much as we can all the time. Think about how long it takes for you to unclench and enjoy a holiday. This is a rest practice for a reason. Our conditioning means it takes time and repetition for us to trust rest.

Restful Moments

You can have restful moments at any time. Here are some examples:

- Gently gazing out of a window, looking at the sky, and taking some deep breaths.

- Stretch your body. You can do this sitting or standing. Take a few mindful breaths.

- Sigh and slowly roll your shoulders back.

- Pay attention to where your body makes contact with whatever you're sitting, standing, or lying on.

- Close your eyes, lay the palms of your hands on your neck, pay attention to how this feels, and take some mindful breaths.

- Slowly eat or drink something and pay attention to all the sensations you experience.

- Lay your hand on your chest and take some slow, deep breaths.

Rest Practice

Our fast-paced lives and a culture that is focused on productive output can make rest feel unsafe. We might use language such as 'I find it hard to rest,' but this hardness is due to us not feeling safe enough to actually do it. Rest for the sake of resting feels lazy and unproductive; for many of us this can feel like a threat, so we resist. This resistance looks like boredom, sensations that feel uncomfortable, an overwhelming urge to put a load of washing on, or wanting to do anything other than resting. This is why this is a rest *practice*.

For a deluxe experience, I recommend using a bolster and two cork yoga blocks.

- Lay one block on its side horizontally and place the other vertically. You will need to adjust according to your height and comfort. I have my blocks about 6in (15cm) apart.

- Then lay the bolster over the blocks, making sure the bolster is a few centimetres over the vertical block. One end of the bolster will be on the vertical block and the other on the floor.

- Sit with the base of your spine right against the part of the bolster on the floor and then lie with your back against the bolster. Feel the front of your body opening and the back softening, soften your shoulders, place your arms in a comfortable position and just lie there.

- If you do not have a bolster and yoga blocks you can simply lie on your bed or sit comfortably.

- Set the timer on your phone for five minutes, allow your eyes to close, pay attention to the rhythm of your breath, and rest.

- Do this three times a week and gradually increase the time to 15 minutes three times a week. If you're unable to rest for the time you set, that's fine. This isn't an exam – it's a practice. The skill is built over time with repetition. If you keep falling asleep it's a sign that you need more sleep.

When I worked full time, I used to do this sitting in my car with the windows ajar. That 15 minutes was golden.

//

CAPACITY VERSUS CAPABILITY

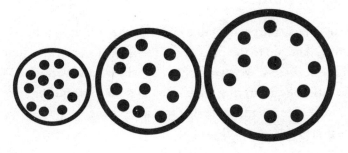

Capacity versus capability

In the image above, the three circles represent your capacity. Each circle has the same number of dots inside and they are all the same size. The largest circle has more space. The dots are not on top of each other and there is space in between them.

When you understand your needs and rhythms and can create healthy boundaries that include the way you care for yourself, it is possible to expand your capacity and widen your window of tolerance.

Let's face it, most of us cannot simply reduce our workload. Modern life is busy. But what we can do is increase our awareness and capacity so that we are not constantly working at maximum capacity and trying to do more on top of that.

Knowing your bandwidth is the key to expanding your bandwidth, but the trick is to expand for spaciousness not to add more, as that is futile. It also undermines the radical act of caring for yourself to a productivity hack and makes the expansions feel like a contraction.

THE INTERSECTIONS OF WOMANHOOD AND YOUR BANDWIDTH

As many of us approach midlife emboldened with new information, we are waking up to the nuances of the gender disparities that still exist in our society. We are questioning why we are working so hard for so little, often carrying the burden of domestic and care work in our homes. We are realizing that this is because the patriarchy still holds power in our world.

But we are not alone in this. These are waters we are all swimming in. Vulnerability and courage are key to creating change because making the changes we need to experience more safety feels like breaking the rules of the psychological contract we are all a part of. Collectively, we must coordinate our efforts to speak out against the systems that oppress us all – the revolution must be organized.

The patriarchy prefers younger women because they are seen as more malleable and less likely to question their conditioning. But as we approach midlife and experience perimenopause and menopause, we become more discerning and no longer want to use our energy to do everything that is projected onto us. As many of us enter this new phase, our mortality becomes more apparent and wisdom refuses to be denied, making itself known through resentment and frustration when we abandon ourselves in favor of 'coping strategies.' This wisdom refuses to be compromised by carrying the burden of household and family responsibilities. This wisdom wants to be wild and free.

It is at this crossroads of women's lives that the patriarchy begins to spread the narrative that women lose their value as they age, making what is normal – aging – seem abnormal. The privilege of life is mocked for doing what it's supposed to, and women fear the inevitable, propping up capitalism with endless purchases of serums and creams to turn back a clock that only moves forward. We must challenge this damaging narrative and recognize that women of all ages have value and are entitled to respect and dignity.

As we navigate midlife and beyond, we gain a deeper understanding of our own bodies and the unique challenges that women face as they age. This knowledge and awareness lead us to become more discerning about how we use our time, particularly in the workplace. We begin to recognize that we have been working as hard as men, but often with significantly less recognition and compensation.

Women hold value at all ages. Our worth is not limited to our childbearing years – we bear fruit in all seasons. By breaking down harmful societal constructs and challenging patriarchal messages that limit women, we can create a more equitable and just society for all. We must make sure that our actions are inclusive, so that we can create a world where age and experience are seen as assets rather than liabilities.

We were born into a world that championed progress and female empowerment. We were raised with the belief that we could conquer any obstacle and achieve our dreams. Glossy magazine after glossy magazine tells us that we can have it all and how. Yet, most women find themselves tangled in a web of traditional gender roles. Society tells us we can be independent, strong, and successful, but the weight of domestic and emotional labor still rests heavily upon our shoulders. The conflicting messages create an impossible set of expectations, leaving us over-functioning on top of overwhelm and googling how to do more tasks in less time, as if it were a time-management issue. This is why many women think differently to their mothers but still relive a version of their lives.

Women strive to excel in their careers/businesses and in their roles as caregivers and homemakers. This looks like taking on the majority of household duties while simultaneously navigating the complexities of the workplace. You tirelessly juggle deadlines, meetings, and presentations, all while ensuring the smooth functioning of your households and trying not to be a nag because you have been gaslighted into believing that the nagging is the issue. The pressure to perform at a high level in both areas is leaving you stretched thin, grappling with exhaustion and the fear of falling short.

It is essential to recognize the toll that these cumbersome responsibilities takes on the modern woman. The exhaustion you experience is not a sign of weakness but a reflection of the immense pressure you experience daily, and the level of resilience you need to survive.

THE INTERSECTION OF WHITE SUPREMACY

Due to the system of white supremacy, women of color face a unique set of challenges. In the workplace and in business, this looks like being overlooked for contracts, promotions, or opportunities due to the intersection of systemic racism and gender-based discrimination. Consequently, Black women need to work harder and longer hours to prove themselves as worthy. The childhood warnings about having to work twice as hard for half the recognition become lived experience. This is evidenced by the racial pay gap.

When Black women try to uphold a boundary, state their needs, or assert themselves, we are often met with the 'angry Black woman' stereotype. This stereotype portrays Black women as overly aggressive, hostile, and difficult to work with, further perpetuating systemic racism and bias. In 2006, my colleagues and I requested a meeting with our head of service because a promised pay rise had not materialized. Everyone was silent so I spoke up and shared that we hadn't received the pay rise and wondered when we would see the increase in our salary. The head of service responded by saying there was a difference between being assertive and aggressive. I wanted the ground to swallow me whole; I was the only person of color in the room and I felt so alone. I immediately began to replay what I had said and how. I was certain that my tone had been polite. I immediately wondered how this might reflect on the other Black staff in my department, as Black people are often treated like a monolith. When we left the meeting with assurances of a back-dated pay rise, three people from the meeting approached me about how unfair our service manager had been and said that I'd been very diplomatic. I wish they had said that in the meeting. I wish I had arranged to see our head of service separately to voice my concerns. This was before terms like 'microaggressions' were common knowledge. I now know I didn't advocate for myself because my survival response is dorsal – to shut down, I was terrified of being judged as having a 'chip on my shoulder.'

When Black women assert themselves, they may be perceived as being 'too demanding,' 'too aggressive,' or 'too emotional,' even if their behavior is no different from their white counterparts'. This double standard can lead to further discrimination and limit their opportunities for growth and progression.

The 'angry Black woman stereotype' is harmful because it reinforces the notion that Black women should be passive and subservient, rather than strong and assertive, even though they are often expected to be strong and aggressive. This creates a vicious circle where Black women are penalized for speaking up, which can limit their ability to advocate for themselves and others.

Moreover, this stereotype can also impact Black women's mental and emotional well-being, as they may feel pressure to suppress their feelings or avoid asserting themselves, so they are not seen as angry or difficult.

I asked a number of Black women on Instagram if they have experiences of not advocating for themselves or not stating their needs because they were concerned about negative stereotypes. The response was yes.

This is the experience of many Black women. It's a pervasive stressor that is often dismissed and internalized. Black women experience this in work and business while being expected to carry a disproportionate amount of the burden of domestic and care work due to their gender, further limiting their time and energy.

PAPERING OVER THE CRACKS WITH RESILIENCE

Throughout our lives, we encounter hardships and face adversity. This is the reality of the human experience. In such times, resilience becomes our anchor, a temporary state of being that enables us to withstand life's challenges and bounce back from difficult events. Resilience, in its essence, is a coping mechanism, a survival instinct that helps us navigate the complexities of life.

However, as I reflect upon resilience and its role in our lives, I cannot help but question the way we have come to perceive and embody it. It has become evident that the gender-biased responsibilities imposed upon women in our society force them into an almost constant state of resilience. For many women, life is an endurance sport, and they are provided with inadequate equipment. It is crucial to recognize that women are not failing at this game; they are playing a system designed for their inevitable loss.

This unrelenting lifestyle leaves women depleted and resentful. They pour their energy and strength into meeting societal expectations, withstanding life's challenges, and being seen to bounce back from difficult times, yet their own well-being is left neglected and unfulfilled. In this situation, women are left to internalize their struggles, turning their pain inward and subjecting themselves to shame and self-blame for not living up to an unrealistic standard of 'being good enough.' Living life like stupid sanitary product adverts in the 90s and 00s, where marketing teams thought women wanted to wear sanitary pads with wings while laughing and playing sports in white shorts.

Resilience should be a temporary measure, a stepping stone towards recovery, enabling us to have an increased capacity and more spaciousness for life where we can experience more joy and authenticity. We must move away from resilience being a lifestyle choice and instead focus on creating a society that promotes genuine well-being and supports the flourishing of women.

Resilience, with its sense of control, often captivates us. As humans conditioned for toxic productivity, we find it difficult to resist the allure of resilience because it keeps us busy and instantly gratifies. However, beneath the surface lies a deeper truth. The allure of false control can prevent us from confronting the pain and exhaustion that hover below the level of consciousness. Women, and in particular Black women, are often afraid to acknowledge their struggles and vulnerabilities, as we know that it will be perceived as weakness or inadequacy.

If we were to pause and truly assess our bandwidth, the capacity of our physical, emotional, and mental resources, we would instead use our unified strength to rise up. Instead of continually piling more onto our plates, we would recognize the importance of setting healthy boundaries and tend to our well-being as though we matter. We would reject the notion that pushing through burnout is a badge of honor and begin to value the rest and restoration we so desperately need.

We wouldn't have to imagine a world where we stop glorifying the depletion of our energy if we stood together to start demanding more for ourselves than fitting into a world that has been dominated by rich white men for the benefit of rich white men. By embracing our limitations instead of being horrified by them and taking stock of our true needs – our bodies' bid for care and connection – we would become catalysts for change. Our courageous acts of self-care and self-advocacy would send ripples throughout society, inspiring future generations of all genders to prioritize their well-being and strive for more harmonious living.

Rest, both physically, emotionally, and spiritually, would become a cherished practice, an act of rebellion against a culture that inflicts perpetual busyness. In honoring our need for rest, we signal to our ancestors that their struggles were not in vain. We create a legacy of joyful resilience rooted in self-compassion, authenticity, and healthy boundaries.

By embracing rest and authenticity, we become role models for future generations. They witness first hand that productivity is a tool used to build success and success will look like the ability to live a life where we can work, rest, and play (Gen X and Xennials, name that advert!). In the words of Marianne Williamson, 'And as we let our own light shine, we unconsciously give other people permission to do the same. As we are liberated from our own fear, our presence automatically liberates others.'[5] We will share our power with younger generations, normalizing a symbiotic relationship between work, rest, and play. Where the idea of work being part of our self-care feels like truth.

Joy Practice

Invite your friends round for a games night! Bring a dish to share or order a takeout. If geographic location is an issue, you can return to 2020 – host a quiz on Zoom or host an online musical bingo night with https://musingobingo.com/.

///

Dear One,

It's time to take the risk of softening enough to admit
that you need to be held and acknowledged, too.

There are gentle hands waiting to embrace you.

If you let them.

If you let you.

CHAPTER 7

CHERISH YOUR CONNECTIONS

'The longer I live, the more deeply I learn
that love — whether we call it friendship
or family or romance — is the work of
mirroring and magnifying each other's
light. Gentle work. Steadfast work. Life-
saving work in those moments when life and
shame and sorrow occlude our own light
from our view, but there is still a clear-eyed
loving person to beam it back. In our best
moments, we are that person for another.'

James Baldwin, *Nothing Personal*

We are innately social creatures. From the earliest days of our existence, we were hardwired for connection, driven by a deep-seated need to belong, to be accepted, and to form meaningful relationships where we can cherish and be cherished. However, the societal structures we've discussed can lead us to stifle our true needs, disrupting our capacity to form these connections.

Our conditioning casts a looming shadow over our ability to forge truly nourishing relationships. The lessons of this world, particularly for girls, often encourage silence over truth. 'Be nice, not honest.' 'Be convenient, don't have needs.' 'Don't cause a scene, be demure.' 'Stop making a fuss; other people have it worse.' 'Your sadness is negative; think positive instead.' Consequently, we learn to deny our rawest emotions, to bury our authentic selves beneath layers of stoicism, positivity, and convenience. What's left is a glossy, compliant veneer that aligns with the prescribed definition of femininity set by the oppressive trinity. You end up living a fragmented life where your truth is so scattered you have difficulty seeing yourself as whole.

The fear of judgment and the common tendency to seek our self-worth from external sources, created by the internalized systems we've come to equate with societal norms, prevent us from revealing the fullness of who we are. We play a perpetual game of hide-and-seek, revealing just enough to keep the game going, but not so much that we risk losing it all. We offer a glimpse, a hint, a shadow of who we *truly* are. We stand behind the veil of fear and doubt, projecting an image that we hope is acceptable, palatable, and 'normal.' The irony is that often, as we refine our personality to please others, we still feel unworthy on the inside. That is until we begin to meet our real selves (see Chapter 4).

The longing for genuine connection is a constant echo in the chambers of our hearts. We yearn for a haven where we can be seen, heard, and held. Relationships that go beyond the superficial, to the very fabric of who we are.

It's my observation that the skill of vulnerability is so under-practiced and therefore underrated that we perceive any real vulnerability as a threat. Consequently, we withhold and withdraw as a means of protection. We don't say, 'I feel like I'm not allowed to be whole when you try to fix me.' We don't say, 'I don't know why I'm scared. Could you hold my hand for a moment, so I don't feel so alone?' We don't say, 'I feel cherished when you make me a cup of tea and look me in my eyes as you hand it to me.' We don't say, 'I don't know the answer, but I'm here to be a compassionate witness and help you remember that your feelings are valid, and you're valuable.'

Instead, we become hypervigilant even in our most-cherished relationships and withdraw from the experiences that make us human – because our lack of emotional competence knocks our confidence and makes us feel vulnerable. We've been conditioned to suppress our emotions and exert excessive control over how we allow ourselves to feel and how we allow ourselves to be seen. This makes the level of vulnerability that supports intimacy seem abnormal and terrifying. It leaves us feeling like we need to protect ourselves from the very thing we need most – connection.

But imagine, for a moment, the liberation we would experience in breaking away from these societal shackles – oh how our cells would rejoice and exhale on behalf of the ancestors that live on in our DNA. What if we dared to express our authentic emotions, regardless of their size or intensity? What if we chose to bare our souls to trusted ones, to be seen and loved for who we truly are – not just the polished, convenient versions of ourselves, but the whole, raw, and vibrant being within?

May we have the courage to reveal our full hand. May we be bold enough to be who we are and create space for others to do the same. May we trust ourselves enough to believe that our emotions in all their grandeur and neediness are not just valid but necessary for our wholeness and our shared human experience. And may we extend this grace to our beloved planet who birthed us all.

Practice Pause

Note: Please don't do this practice if you're driving, operating machinery or doing anything that requires your attention.

- Let's take a moment here to be with whatever wants to arise. If you can, lie flat on the ground with your feet flat on the floor, so your knees are bent and your lower back is supported. If you're unable to lie on the floor, sit comfortably or stand with your feet hip distance apart and soften your knees so you're not rigid. If it feels good to do so, I invite you to gently close your eyes. If not, look ahead and soften your gaze so the outside world becomes a blur.

- Feel the connection between your body and the ground beneath you. Remember that the ground you're lying, sitting, or standing on is held by the Earth; therefore, you are held by the Earth. Connect with your breath without altering it. Just take note of the air entering and leaving your body and see if paying attention to your breath changes it.

- On your next exhale, see if you can allow yourself to soften into the ground a little more. Allow yourself to feel heavy, to let go. Pay attention to the Earth rising to meet you, holding the weight of your body as much as you allow, giving you as much as you're willing to receive. On your next exhale, put one hand on your chest and the other on your tummy. Feel your body rise and fall with each breath. Now I want you to pay attention to how it feels to be held, just as you are.

- Now I invite you to think about something you need from your important relationships right now and don't judge yourself for it. I'll be honest with you: what I'm craving in this moment is more validation and recognition, and despite the tinge of self-judgment, I'm owning it. If you can't think of a thing right now, that's just fine. Your thing will make itself known in due time. Bring your attention back to your connection with the ground, and now ask the Earth to meet this need, imagine this need being fully met in this moment. Allow yourself to receive what the Earth has to offer and be here with whatever arises. If you find yourself switching off, imagine yourself breathing in what you need on each inhalation.

- How does it feel to state your need? How does it feel to allow yourself to be vulnerable in the presence of the Earth? How does it feel to show your hand and allow it to be seen?

- Now bring your attention back to your connection with the ground and allow your eyes to gently open. You may wish to journal in response to the prompts above.

//

FROM SELF-REJECTION TO SELF-ACCEPTANCE: A PERSONAL JOURNEY

Suppressing the qualities we have been conditioned to deem as 'too much' often precipitates a sense of inadequacy, a feeling of not being 'enough.' We end up preemptively rejecting ourselves before we can be rejected by others, further perpetuating this feeling of not-enoughness. Swinging like a pendulum between being overwhelmed by how much we need and feeling unworthy of having our needs met. In my personal journey, this manifested as splitting off from parts of myself, casting aside the fragments that did not suit the 'strong independent' stereotype I thought I had to inhabit, only to envy those around me who embodied the very traits I had banished. The irony wasn't lost on me: in my performance of strength and independence, I found myself filled with incandescent irritation directed toward friends I judged as 'needy,' while I literally worked tirelessly to reject my own needs in the name of being strong and independent. I was battling an internal war and silently waging it against others in the form of passive-aggressive behavior, criticism dressed as advice, and bitterness I tried my best to swallow. My own poisoned chalice.

This internal tug-of-war became starkly evident to me in 2017, when my coach and now friend, Nicola Rae, welcomed me into her coaching program. Among the beautiful materials in the welcome pack were affirmation cards, one of which read, 'Today I'll be my own best friend.' The card triggered a visceral response, almost akin to repulsion. It was as if the part of me that yearned for my friendship was simultaneously recoiling at the notion of it, feeling small and undeserving. This ambivalence – the simultaneous desire for my own friendship and the fear of what it might reveal – marked a period of palpable discomfort, necessitating years of therapy for me to understand and begin to address.

This journey of introspection and healing highlighted the fact that being 'too much' or 'too needy' is not weak, but a testament to our human need for connection and support. It's about being whole in a world that often asks us to fragment ourselves. And it is in embracing this wholeness that we can become our own best friends – accepting, loving, and supporting ourselves through the kaleidoscope of experiences that constitute our human journey.

THE HEALING POWER OF AUTHENTIC RELATIONSHIPS

'Connection is a biological imperative – a
need that must be met to sustain life.'

Deb Dana

Despite our conditioning, we are hardwired for connection and this hardwiring always prevails. As such, I've been privileged to experience the profoundly healing power of relationships that offer enough space for you to reveal your true self. These relationships are rare sanctuaries in the tumultuous landscape of life – havens that allow us to speak what we believe to be unspeakable and be held tenderly.

They are not all close, intimate relationships but they are relationships that include some closeness and intimacy. For example, your pal at work who supports your ideas in meetings, will rage-check your emails before you press send, and give you a heads-up when shit's about to hit the fan. Or your neighbor's children, whose eyes light up when they see you in the neighborhood. Interactions we overlook in the busyness of our lives that make our hearts flutter with gratitude when we take a moment and pay attention. This is what it is to be human, and these experiences become more widely available when our needs are met enough for us to connect as such. These glimmers foster a neuroception of safety that says you're part of something bigger, you're not alone. And this reminds us that a lot of what we strive for is simply waiting for us to connect with it.

Imagine stepping into a space filled with kindness and acceptance, where your most profound fears and most exuberant joys are met with the gentlest of gazes. A place where the soothing cadence of a voice can act as a balm for the turmoil within; where time seems to stretch, providing room for stories untold and emotions unexpressed.

In these spaces, you're met with a response that's nothing short of an empathetic embrace, a response that says, 'I'm here. I'm present. I'm ready to listen to you.' In these moments, the seemingly impenetrable walls we build around ourselves start to crumble. The masks we wear start to slip. The authentic self, in all its raw beauty, begins to peek through.

These relationships are transformational, not just because they allow us to express ourselves without judgment, but because they teach us about the power of vulnerability. It's here we understand that revealing what's below the tip of the iceberg – our joys, our fears, our aspirations, our regrets – is not an act of weakness, but one of courage. Not a display of brokenness that needs repair, but a testament to our bravery. These relationships are an act of reclaiming our identity from societal expectations and redefining it on our terms. Liberating us from the trap of toxic productivity so we can find our joy.

The experience of being seen and heard in our entirety is deeply therapeutic. It tells us we are enough just as we are: no pretense, no posturing – just pure and genuine, a reflection of nature, made in the vision of the Divine. It's in these relationships that we realize our 'too much' and 'not enough' are part of our whole, and we need not disown any part of ourselves to belong. And as we do this for ourselves, we naturally do the same for others.

The healing power of such relationships cannot be understated. They shape our perception of self and others. They support us to be courageous enough to belong to ourselves and embrace ourselves as we are. And they teach us the profound value of being human. No accolades, efficiency, or profit margins can do that.

These relationships are not as rare as they may seem. I have held spaces and witnessed the way authentic connection sets a precedent for how we can, and should, engage with ourselves and the world around us. These relationships teach us that at the heart of meaningful relationships is the ability to be imperfectly human and the willingness to allow others to be the same. In my work, I host events and spaces where women gather, from online group work, women's circles, and exploration salons where we explore relevant topics, to in-person retreats and events. The space I hold has been described as a place where the nervous system can rest.

When we gather in these spaces, regardless of the content we share, the spaces are ventral because of our shared experience, collective empathy, and willingness to listen, so we can hear and know the person before us. This is the power of co-regulation, where our nervous systems sense signs of safety in the nervous systems around us and give us permission to settle.

> *'The first part of emotional healing is being*
> *limbically known – having someone with a*
> *keen ear catch your melodic essence.'*
>
> **Thomas Lewis,** *A General Theory of Love*

In spaces where you're met with love, the stress caused by the capitalist narrative of independence, individualism, and being self-sufficient and the personal experiences of trauma are soothed because, as bell hooks taught us, healing is an act of communion. As the most social creatures on this planet, we do not heal in isolation, contrary to what the term 'self-help' might imply. Our healing work often begins in isolation, but to a degree, this part is like the theory. The theory is tested by our interactions with the real world.

UBUNTU – I AM BECAUSE WE ARE (WE ARE BECAUSE YOU ARE)

Ubuntu is a Nguni Bantu term from Southern Africa that roughly translates to 'humanity' or 'humanity towards others.' It's a philosophy or worldview that emphasizes the interconnectedness and interdependence of all human beings. Ubuntu embraces compassion, kindness, empathy, and respect for others, and it is often expressed through the phrase 'I am because we are.' In essence, Ubuntu means that we are all connected and that our well-being and happiness are dependent on the well-being and happiness of others.

According to anthropologist Margaret Mead, the first evidence of human civilization was a 15,000-year-old fractured femur bone that had healed.[1] The femur is the thigh bone; it's the longest and strongest bone in the human body and plays a vital role in us being able to stand and move. The bone was found on an archaeological site and Mead hypothesized that this was evidence of someone or a group of people taking time to stay with a wounded person, binding their leg, carrying the person to a place of safety, and supporting their healing. Mead further explained that breaking your leg in the animal kingdom meant you would die as you would be too impaired to keep yourself safe from other tribes or predatory animals. Hunting for food and finding water would be more challenging. If Mead's educated guess is correct, this is an example of where courage and compassion create a powerful force that motivates people to take action and help others, even if it places them at risk.

'A broken femur that has healed is evidence that
another person has taken time to stay with the fallen,
has bound up the wound, has carried the person to
safety and has tended them through recovery.'
Margaret Mead

According to this story, at least one human being risked their life to save the life of another and assumed the extra responsibility of providing shelter and sustenance for the wounded person to stay alive. This is courage and compassion in action. I would imagine that the logical mind was terrified, but the heart took over like the powerful force of nature it is. Courage and compassion are embodied; they require a great deal of self-awareness and mindfulness. They involve acknowledging and accepting your own vulnerability and finding the inner strength and resilience to face challenges. This requires an awareness of your body that allows you to feel and be present with internal sensations long enough to trust them as wise advisers. It means feeling your feelings and, for a society that has been taught that feelings of vulnerability are a weakness, even mild sensations can feel overwhelming.

Cherish Practice

In our culture of toxic productivity, cherishing ourselves, our loved ones, and our planet is an arduous task because it contradicts our unconscious social contract; that productivity and worth are interlinked, self-sacrifice is noble, and vulnerability is weak. This makes the act of love in the everyday not only a rebellion but a courageous act of defiance. Raised to be obedient rather than courageous, we need to cultivate the ability to cherish, nurture, and care for lovingly.

Cherish: verb – protect and care for (someone) lovingly.

Synonyms: Treasure, adore, hold dear, nurture, value, appreciate, nourish, respect, delight in, enjoy, fancy, like.

This word denotes being an active steward in fostering love, care, and respect. But how often do we apply this to ourselves and our relationships?

Reflect on These Questions

When was the last time you:

- Delighted in your own existence?

- Held yourself dear?

- Treasured your quirks and eccentricities?

- How do you show appreciation to yourself, not just for what you do or achieve, but for simply being you?

Now, extend this inquiry to your relationships. How often do you:

- Delight in the company of those you care for?

- When was the last time you let them know just how dear they are to you?

- What do you treasure in your loved ones, the attributes that make them unique? How do you express your appreciation for their presence in your life?

Now answer these questions about yourself:

- What delights you about yourself?

- Which of your qualities do you hold dear and what is precious about you?

- What do you treasure about yourself? How can you treasure this more often?

- What do you appreciate about yourself – not your accomplishments or actions, but the simple, profound things that make you, you?

- Are there practices you can develop to cherish yourself more fully?

And for your adult relationships, bring to mind someone you would like to cherish more:

- What delights you about this person?

- Which of their qualities do you hold dear and what is precious about them?

- What do you treasure about this person? How can you treasure this more often?

- What do you appreciate about this person – not their accomplishments or actions, but the simple, profound things that make them who they are?

- What small steps can you take to cherish this person more often?

I must take a moment to share one of my mum's responses:

'I treasure my determination to go outside my comfort zone. Always thriving and never giving in to that feeling of imposter syndrome. Life without that extra effort is boring so striving to achieve self-satisfaction, inner health, and wealth not in materialistic ways but to have peace of mind that you can thrive, delight, love, laugh, enjoy, and play. In that Salone* notion that life should be about enjoyment. Your day-to-day life should tickle every emotion, bones and muscles of your life.'

Cecilia Thomas

- Next, I invite you to create an affirmation based on one of your responses about yourself; an example based on my mum's response might be, *'I treasure my courage to step beyond my comfort zone and my ability to love, laugh, and enjoy life.'*

- To make this embodied, I recommend going on an affirmation breath walk. During this walk, inhale to the count of four and then exhale to the count of four and repeat. Get into a rhythm with this breath. Once you find your rhythm repeat your affirmation for two minutes. Return to your normal breathing pattern and repeat the affirmations loud enough for you to hear – don't worry about how you may look, people will assume you're on the phone. Repeat this five times for an exhilarating experience.

///

---

* Salone is a nickname for Sierra Leone.

AUTHENTIC RELATIONSHIPS ARE REGENERATIVE

While capitalism is degenerative, authentic relationships are regenerative. Capitalism focuses on continuous growth for the sake of individual gain, and the hoarding of wealth that only benefits the few. In this pursuit, capitalism gives precedence to transactional relationships, where interactions are driven by self-interest, productivity, and profit. In a society that is structured around the work we do to create a 'living,' there is limited time and space for meaningful connection and this limitation is fodder for capitalism.

Just think about all the abandoned plans in the group chat because people's packed-full diaries have no space for enjoyment without a purpose. Weddings? Yes, worth the rearranging, usually plenty of notice, and an honor to be invited. Birthdays? Maybe, depending on who and where. As we get older, it may also depend on whether it's a 'significant' birthday or not. Also, when it comes to social engagements, we are all so needy due to the limited time we have for pleasure that the stakes are too bloody high.

I have often found myself calculating whether or not the two hours at dinner (it's always dinner!) are going to be worth prepping dinner for my daughter, getting dressed, putting on makeup, power walking to the Tube, two hours travel there and back, the best part of £100 (and still coming home hungry), the awkwardness of pointing out that I don't drink alcohol when the bill comes, and thinking about how tired I'm going to be tomorrow! I know I sound like Scrooge, but when working makes time so finite, even enjoyment can feel like a chore.

I often think about all the good ideas that got abandoned because no one has the energy to coordinate all the ravenous needs that beg to be met in one social event. Think about the relief we sometimes

IN A SOCIETY THAT IS
STRUCTURED AROUND THE
WORK WE DO TO CREATE A
'LIVING,' THERE IS LIMITED
TIME AND SPACE FOR
MEANINGFUL CONNECTION
AND THIS LIMITATION IS
FODDER FOR CAPITALISM.

(often) feel when social plans are canceled because though we may have had good intentions when we said yes to the invite in the first place, we didn't have the energy to follow through when the day of the event arrived.

> *'But in the end the most significant aspect of play is*
> *that it allows us to express our joy and connect most*
> *deeply with the best in ourselves, and in others. If your*
> *life has become barren, play brings it to life again.*
> *Yes, as Freud said, life is about love and work. Yet play*
> *transcends these, infuses them with liveliness and stills*
> *time's arrow. Play is the purest expression of love.'*
>
> **Dr. Stuart Brown, *Play***

Capitalism celebrates perpetual economic expansion while neglecting the essential elements of rest, connection, and space needed for genuine personal growth. Relationships built on a meaningful connection where we feel safe to be intimate can appear to be fruitless because there is often no commodifiable outcome. Furthermore, they can feel unsafe because we do not get the opportunity to build the skill of relating to each other as human beings with a complex and beautiful array of characteristics that make us whole. However, it is in these relationships that we get to be human beings.

INTERNALIZED MISOGYNY

Nestled within the intricate interplay of the oppressive trinity is a subtle, insidious phenomenon that can profoundly impact our emotional landscapes: internalized misogyny. It's a product of long-standing gender norms that define 'masculinity' and 'femininity' in narrow, limiting terms. As skillfully explored in the book *Feminism for the 99% – A Manifesto*, these limiting terms are in messages about women 'leaning in' and buying into 'equal opportunity domination' instead of calling for changes to be made so that the system becomes more equitable for all. The book explains that the effects of patriarchal dominance do not have to be perpetuated by a man. Similarly, other forms of discrimination can be internalized and projected outward.[2]

Our societal fabric weaves compelling narratives about how men should behave – valuing traits like strength, stoicism, competitiveness, self-reliance – and flagging these as 'masculine.' In contrast, qualities considered 'feminine' such as emotional expressiveness, empathy, vulnerability, nurturing, are often side-lined or rejected outright. As men navigate this conditioning, they can end up distancing themselves from any qualities they perceive as 'feminine,' limiting their emotional range and capacity for deep connections.

The racial dimension of white supremacy further complicates this situation. Men of color, especially Black men, are subject to additional pressures to conform to 'masculine' behaviors, often as a means of survival against the prejudiced stereotypes placed upon them. These further fuel the internalized misogyny, tightening its stranglehold on emotional capacity and deep, intimate connection.

Internalized misogyny occurs when societal narratives that devalue and disparage 'femininity' are absorbed and reflected in behavior and interactions. It can seep into our consciousness subtly, expressing itself through unconscious biases, or more overtly, through hostility towards women and 'feminine' traits. For men, it engenders internal conflict – a battle with self-acceptance – where societal narratives promote the rejection of anything associated with femininity within their own identities. The repercussions of this struggle can be deep-seated, stifling emotional growth and the capacity for vulnerability, empathy, and emotional connection.

At this point, we must stop and ask ourselves: How does this serve us? Do rigid gender roles and dismissal of 'feminine' qualities benefit our emotional well-being and relationships? Or do they constrain us, causing us to reject parts of ourselves, limiting our capacity for empathy, vulnerability, and deep emotional connections?

While researching this book, I found myself deep down TikTok rabbit holes of content creators and podcasters sharing what I experienced as prehistoric views on the need for men to be providers and women to be subservient. There are content creators with massive platforms teaching women how to 'be in their feminine energy' and men how to 'be in their masculine.' Despite being cognitively alarmed by this, I must confess that, deep down I'm attracted to the idea of a male partner who earns more than me and who remains calm in the midst of panic. That said, he'd better not dare think he can tell me what to do! I don't know if this is nature or nurture, but I'm sure that this is the 'yes and' aspect of being human. This speaks to the at times complex contradiction of life. While I'm alarmed at most of the conditions imposed by traditional gender roles, I'm still emotionally attracted to some of them. I reject the misogyny of patriarchy and desire some 'traditionally' masculine qualities.

It would be much easier, superficially, for me to reject these feelings because I reject misogyny and how the system of capitalism thrives on it. But if I reject these feelings then I just fall into the trap of rejecting myself again, whereas when I welcome all my emotions, I can not only be more honest with myself but also with others.

If we take a moment to meditate on this introspection, we can realize that this is not destiny, it is a matter of unlearning. Unlearning these binary gender expectations that serve only to confine our emotional landscapes into Stepford-style gardens. Unlearning the narratives that associate vulnerability and empathy with weakness. Unlearning the conditioning that stifles emotional expressiveness is the path to justice and true equality. We must collectively unlearn our conditioning and not rush to create something new; we must take a moment to be with what we find within ourselves and each other and use this to create something new, something true.

> 'We will not end white-body supremacy – or any other
> form of human evil – by trying to tear it to pieces.
> Instead, we can offer people better ways to belong,
> and better things to belong to. Instead of belonging
> to a race, we can belong to a culture. Each of us can
> also build our own capacity for genuine belonging.'
>
> **Resmaa Menakem,** *My Grandmother's Hands*

The systems of oppression have to operate at a fast pace so that we do not feel. Our unlearning must be paced so that we may feel, heal, release, and rebirth.

As we embark on this journey of unlearning, we also embark on a journey of redefining – redefining societal notions of strength and success to include emotional intelligence, empathy, and vulnerability. By acknowledging the inherent value in these traditionally 'feminine' qualities, we begin to dismantle internalized misogyny and the limitations it places on emotional capacity. This will offer us a more caring and regenerative way to belong.

This redefinition opens the door to a new form of connection, one that acknowledges the full spectrum of human emotion, offering space for people to express their true selves, unbound by societal stereotypes. It allows us to form deeper, meaningful connections, connections that are grounded in authenticity, compassion, and a shared human experience.

When we embrace this holistic view of personhood, it is possible to see that we are not just 'masculine' or 'feminine.' We are human beings, capable of a broad range of emotions, experiences, and connections. The realization of this wholeness is the antidote to the constraints of internalized misogyny. It's a path toward a more compassionate society, a society that values authenticity, emotional expressiveness, and deep connections. A rooted society that celebrates us, in our entirety.

AUTHENTICITY AND ABUNDANCE

In authentic relationships, people recognize and honor the inherent worth and dignity of each other. They understand that their well-being is interconnected and that by nurturing these relationships, they contribute to the greater ecosystem of life. Like the interconnectedness found in nature, authentic relationships create a web of support, love, and understanding that radiates outward, positively impacting people, communities, and our planet.

Unlike capitalism, which is characterized by scarcity and competition, authentic relationships follow a distinct pattern that embraces abundance, collaboration, and the knowledge that by working together, we can collectively thrive. These relationships cultivate trust, emotional safety, and a sense of belonging, providing fertile ground for personal growth, resilience, and fulfillment.

These relationships support social justice, which means the pursuit of equal rights for all and creating an equitable society where everyone has the chance to thrive.

By emphasizing authentic relationships, we shift our focus from hyper-individualism to nurturing connections that enrich and regenerate the ecosystem of life. Instead of extracting from others or the environment, we actively contribute to the well-being of ourselves, others, and the world around us.

In this regenerative framework, authentic relationships become a force for positive change. They are a fertile ground for empathy, compassion, and social cohesion, leading to collective well-being and the restoration of our shared humanity.

THE DOMINANT SUFFER, TOO

Throughout this book, I have shared the different ways the trinity of oppression permeates our lives as individuals and as a collective, and how they exert substantial influence on our emotional well-being and our capacity for intimacy. The impact of these systems is profound, and for most men, these influences limit their ability to maintain caring relationships where they get to be vulnerable, tender, caring, and cared for. The 'cared for' I'm talking about is not caretaking, it is about them having relational spaces where they feel safe enough to take the risk of being a full-spectrum human.

Under the dominion of capitalism, the relentless pressure to succeed economically and the ensuing culture of constant competition ravages personal well-being. In a society that equates worth with wealth, emotions are deemed as distractions, a sign of weakness that will derail us from the track of economic success. Under this system men are disadvantaged because they are expected to suppress their vulnerability and emotional expression, hindering their emotional growth and capacity for deep, caring relationships. White supremacy, a malignant belief system underpinned by prejudice and discrimination, further deepens these fissures in our ecosystem. The singular 'ideal' of worth or success being defined by masculine, white, Western culture obstructs the emotional growth of those who are perceived to fall short of this 'ideal.' The incessant need to 'prove their worth and provide' can stunt emotional openness, further limiting the capacity for intimacy. This struggle keeps all of us stuck in a constant state of survival so our bodies' neuroception is constantly picking up signs of danger and reacting accordingly. The emotional ineptitude created by the stoicism of white supremacy means that many men are suspicious of intimate care and love, as it is impossible to treat people in inhumane ways without being inhumane to yourself. Under capitalism, the mistreatment of humans is exchanged for profit; in order to sustain this, emotions and the felt sense must be denied. As we learned from Brené Brown, emotions and the felt sense cannot be shut off in a piecemeal fashion. Consequently, the essential, primal biological need for care becomes a suspicious shadow concealing all the needs that have been abandoned in pursuit of success.

People who are marginalized usually have access to fewer resources and are therefore unable to pay for sophisticated means of defense such as lobbying parliament or donating to a political party. People who are marginalized usually have to use their bodies as their defense mechanism – as this is what they have access to. This looks like striking, protest marches, and sit-ins – things that people with access to financial and societal resources tell us are aggressive, uncivilized, and uncouth. For example, the vigil held in the UK for Sarah Everard, who was kidnapped, raped, and murdered by a serving police officer – a position that benefits from all three aspects of the oppressive trinity. The gathering of women paying their respects was reported to have been met with a heavy-handed response by the police. I also cannot mention this without acknowledging that two women of color, Bibaa Henry and her sister Nicole Smallman, were also murdered nine months prior to this with only a fraction of the rightful outrage and declarations of support for Sarah Everard, a blatant display of white supremacy, even in the midst of tragedy. It's a beast that never sleeps.

In relation to the matter of civility one must ask, what is civilized about using money and influence to maintain a system that discriminates against so many?

Patriarchy emphasizes traditional 'masculine' behaviors such as emotional stoicism and dominance, which erodes men's capacity for vulnerability. Emotional expression, a cornerstone of deep and intimate connections, is frequently discouraged, placing yet another constraint on the ability to form affectionate relationships and placing the weight of emotionality on women, while criticizing women for being too emotional, hormonal, or hysterical. Gaslighting them for taking up the slack left by men who have been conditioned to abandon their humanity for the spoils of ambition.

The interplay of these structures amplifies their individual impacts. Men living under this triple shadow of capitalism, white supremacy, and patriarchy find themselves caught in a pressurized vault of suppressed emotions, relentless economic pressures, and stringent societal expectations contributing to the worrying rate of suicide among men. According to independent mental health provider The Priory, women are more likely to attempt suicide, but men account for 74 percent of all suicides in the UK.[3] This is a devastating statistic, and I cannot help but wonder how many lives would be preserved if our emotional lives were handled with more grace and care.

These societal structures don't impact all men uniformly, however, and it would be remiss to overlook the significant influence they have on us all. Individual experiences, identities, and contexts substantially shape how these structures influence our emotional well-being and capacity for intimacy, but we must acknowledge that these systems taint the water we are all swimming in.

However, there is hope. There is always hope. We are sentient beings with the ability to change and be changed; our evolution is proof of this. We have demonstrated time and time again that we have a potent counterforce, the transformative power of love. Far from a mere sentiment, love can be a conduit for empathy, a catalyst for emotional well-being, and a cradle for nurturing deep, caring relationships.

What if we reimagined productivity not as a measure of economic output, but as an embodiment of love and care? This paradigm shift can challenge the limitations imposed by capitalism, white supremacy, and patriarchy. By placing love at the center, we recognize its power to inspire action, to effect positive outcomes, and to catalyse personal growth, all things we try to achieve with toxic productivity because we have been conditioned to believe that financial success is a panacea for these things.

Through the act of love, we learn to hear others, to see them for who they truly are, and to genuinely value their presence, flaws and all. Love creates an environment that fosters trust, collaboration, and deeper connections. Moreover, it equips us to navigate the complexities of life with grace and compassion.

Joy Practice

For this practice, I'm tapping into an unmet childhood wish. When I was a child, I wanted a pen pal. I never did anything about it! So, I'm going to indulge my inner child and bring you with me. For this joy practice, I invite you to hand write and post a letter to a friend telling them why your friendship with them is revolutionary.

Next, I want you to write an email to yourself telling you why your relationship with you is revolutionary. Don't send it immediately – schedule it to be delivered one year from now.

///

Dear One

Before we delve into this chapter, I want to
acknowledge your courage and commitment.

This material is not easy reading.

It's as confronting as it is comforting.

This journey has been about understanding
how we got here and how we had to adapt in
order to survive, often at the expense of our
life-force energy, safety, and authenticity.

CHAPTER 8
CHOOSING YOU

*'True belonging is the spiritual practice of
believing and belonging to yourself so deeply that
you can share your most authentic self with the
world and find sacredness in both being a part of
something and standing alone in the wilderness.
True belonging doesn't require you to change
who you are; it requires you to be who you are.'*

Brené Brown

B ecoming acquainted with your nervous system might have been a confronting task, highlighting the reality that despite your accomplishments, you've been operating in survival mode. However, there is great power and comfort in knowing that you have the ability to nurture yourself and become your greatest advocate by becoming a friend to your nervous system. This is a highly sophisticated skill that promotes connection with the nervous systems of those around us through the process of co-regulation. It's the combined energy of co-regulation that becomes a catalyst for societal change.

What you've read so far may have evoked a cocktail of emotions, including righteous rage or sorrow about societal conventions that normalize forsaking our humanity in the relentless pursuit of productivity and external validation – benchmarks we have been taught to use as a measure of our worth.

In meeting the real you it's possible that you were alerted to the ways you've learned to internalize oppressive behavior, thereby contributing to your harm. However, in understanding our natural inclination for productivity and that our bandwidth holds powerful data, you may have felt a sense of relief as you acknowledge that you're not inconsistent or inefficient – you're designed to wax and wane.

In becoming a friend to your nervous system and reading about the revolutionary power of relationships, I hope you're reassured that your needs don't make you 'needy.' They are a natural bid for connection, part of the genius of our species that encourages us to choose ourselves and find others who can do the same.

CHOOSING YOU IS NOT SELFISH

Societal transformation begins with individual transformation. The act of choosing yourself, particularly for women and, even more critically, for women of color, is a vital catalyst in sparking meaningful change.

Choosing yourself is not an act of self-interest or selfishness; it involves a profound understanding and reclamation of our emotional and psychological needs. Our oppressive system is based on choosing the self at the expense of the other because it is a system based on 'power over' as set out in Chapter 1. This is hierarchical and used to dominate and exploit, which enables a powerful few to control resources and manufacture scarcity for profit. An alternative is power that is gracious enough to be distributed and shared instead of hoarded. This can be achieved through appropriate compensation for workers; care work and emotional labor being recognized as the backbone of society and supported as such; a taxation system that supports social welfare instead of corporations; and systems of care being at the center of everything we do. We do not need more billionaires – we need more care.

To do this, we must learn to choose ourselves, so we understand ourselves and therefore have the capacity to choose and understand others. The late, great Audre Lorde taught us that caring for ourselves is not self-indulgence, 'it is self-preservation and that is an act of political warfare.'[1] Consciously choosing ourselves – our whole selves, not just the parts we are rewarded for – is a radical act that gives us permission to prioritize our emotional and psychological safety so that we may feel grounded enough to take the risk of truly living and have the capacity to allow others to do the same.

As can be seen in my 360-system care model (below), embodying this level of safety creates a ripple effect where safety leads to regulation (both co- and self-). When our need for regulation is met, it naturally evolves into resilience. Resilience leads to an increased capacity. If we don't fill this increased capacity with busyness, it creates space, which enables us to make conscious choices rather than just survive.

The 360-system care model

With this in place, self-care becomes restorative rather than a means to patch up the wounds of survival. When we are able to nourish ourselves with care, we naturally care for others. This is hardwired in our DNA and it leads to social care.

Social care that is underpinned by this framework creates an environment for social justice because we will no longer be overwhelmed by any dominant power that seeks to extract for its own benefit. And this creates a system based on care where we are citizens making a valuable contribution, rather than commodities to be exploited for capital.

This requires conscious choices that go against the grain of our conditioning. Creating this friction will cause a chain reaction of progress starting from a foundation of emotional safety, and emotional safety requires the courageous act of choosing oneself when it feels safer to self-abandon. Here are some ways self-abandonment happens:

- **Ignoring feelings:** Pushing aside your own emotions or pretending you're fine when you're not.

- **People-pleasing:** Always doing what you think others want you to do, even if it makes you unhappy or uncomfortable.

- **Overworking:** Focusing so much on work or 'productive' tasks that you forget to take care of yourself or feel like you have to work hard to earn the right to care for yourself.

- **Sacrificing for others:** Constantly putting other people's needs before your own without considering what you need.

- **Staying quiet:** Not speaking up when something bothers you or when you disagree with others.

- **Faking perfection:** Trying to appear perfect and hiding your flaws or mistakes to seek approval from others.

- **Ignoring boundaries:** Allowing others to disrespect your personal space or take advantage of you.

- **Suppressing aspirations:** Putting aside your ambitions or dreams because you think they're not important, because someone else might disapprove, or you fear change.

- **Staying in situations that don't serve you:** Remaining in unhealthy relationships, jobs, or environments because you're afraid to leave.

- **Avoiding self-care:** Neglecting fundamental self-care routines, like eating well, exercising, or getting enough sleep, because you're too focused on other things or people.

- **Denying true self:** Hiding your real thoughts, feelings, or identity because you're afraid of what people might think.

- **Ignoring intuition:** Not listening to your gut feeling or inner voice, even when it tells you something is wrong.

We must trust that as the most pro-social creatures on this planet, choosing ourselves and prioritizing self-care organically expands into social care, nurturing a society rooted in empathy, respect, and social justice.

> *'Nurturing your own development isn't selfish.*
> *It's actually a great gift to other people.'*
> **Rick Hanson**

Beginning with safety is essential, as choosing you cannot happen in a vacuum. It will unfold amid the pervasive systemic structures of white supremacy, patriarchy, and capitalism. It will unravel your relationships, which can pose significant challenges.

As a Black woman with rich dark skin, choosing me has required confronting deeply ingrained biases. I've faced criticism from Black friends who, when I made the conscious decision to embrace my natural hair texture, expressed a preference for my hair when it was chemically straightened. I've had to consciously reclaim my beauty in a world that often negates it – seemingly surface-level harm that wounds deep into my core. An injury that is so profound it tells me that I was born fundamentally flawed because I do not reflect white supremacist beauty standards.

Choosing myself requires me to affirm my identity and actively reject the harmful narrative that my natural state is a deviation from what is considered 'beautiful' when, in truth, I'm a reflection of the Divine. It's been about navigating my way through the disquieting waters of societal bias and learning to stand firm in my inherent worth, so that I may know my beauty every single day. This journey is fraught with challenges, but it is a journey I must endure in a society that tells me I'm anything but pure.

I face racism in so many ways, from white people who think they are well meaning wanting me to consider both sides, and liberal white women who want me to prioritize their comfort over my emotional safety, to witnessing the way the world treats people who look like me with disdain. This can look like microaggressions such as comments about how articulate I am; sharing pictures, videos and images of Black people being harmed without thinking about how this content could cause me harm; or expecting me to use my platform to speak about every issue that impacts Black people. It's also well-meaning white women 'all lives mattering' topics when they are specifically about Black women. For example, when talking about the strong Black woman stereotype, I'm often met by white women who believe that the strong woman trope is universal. While there are commonalities, the intersection of race adds more layers of complexity, as I have highlighted throughout this book. I'm visible, educated, articulate, and well spoken. This makes me a palatable Black woman. Consequently, people can attempt to tokenize me, as I'm good for 'diversity' metrics.

Choosing ourselves means pushing against a narrative that has created an environment where we are 'more likely to experience belittling microaggressions, such as having our judgement questioned or being mistaken for someone more junior.'[2] It includes speaking our truth, even when it means potentially being ostracized.

> *'When a man speaks assertively, people trust him:*
> *he's confident. When a woman does it, men dislike*
> *her: she's a bitch. It's outrageous that women have*
> *to tame their tongues to protect fragile egos.'*
>
> **Adam Grant**

Choosing myself has meant being civil to abusive, intoxicated men on the last train home because I fear what might happen if my refusal creates embarrassment. Or the painstaking task of having to explain why it is unfair and unreasonable to expect women to do most of the caretaking and emotional labor everywhere.

Under capitalism, where profit is prioritized over people and planet while self-interest and competition is incentivized to the detriment of communal well-being, choosing yourself can feel like perpetuating the same problem. However, it's essential not to confuse this with the pressure and stress caused by the economic inequality created by capitalism, as it undermines emotional safety and impedes our ability to make conscious, self-affirming choices. What I'm talking about here is not choosing yourself via the fancy bubble bath aisle in a department store or escaping from life at a yoga retreat (although these things have their place). I'm talking about choosing yourself as the first step of radical self-care that enables us to shift to social care based on empathy, cooperation, and collective welfare that will become the foundation of a culture that is socially just.

So, you see, choosing yourself is not an insular act. It is a reclamation that enables us to be in right relationship with ourselves, so we have the capacity to extend that to others and our planet. This is a revolutionary act of love and care that doubles up as a powerful rebellion against a system designed for us to mistrust ourselves, so we forget who we are and whose we are; so that we don't recognize our own agency. We are the daughters of the Earth; our evolution is a force of nature, and it starts with us proudly choosing ourselves rather than waiting to be chosen by a system designed to suspend us in a perpetual state of survival.

The oppressive trinity thrives on disconnection and a lack of belonging that creates the illusion that we are separate from each other rather than individual parts of one whole, one ecosystem. These systems create hierarchies that thrive on the exploitation of people who are marginalized. They are a stark contrast to our innate need for connection and belonging.

As Toni Morrison remarked, 'If you can only be tall when somebody else is on their knees, then you've got a serious problem.'[3] We do indeed have a very serious problem, which can be ameliorated by learning who we are and what we need to feel safe with ourselves and each other.

Choosing you requires a level of accountability that can feel exposing. While I'm an advocate for reframing the way we perceive our needs, the undeniable truth is that sometimes we can be too demanding and too much for others because we are subconsciously projecting our unmet needs onto them. This pattern makes our personal responsibility become someone else's burden. Generally speaking, taking time and space to connect with the foundations of who you are and what you need is not taught, or role modeled. In fact, we are often urged to dismiss our foundational needs so that we can be productive and convenient. Consequently, we find it difficult to accept our needs and instead project them outward. Our need for support manifests as caring for others; our longing for intimacy becomes providing intimacy for others; our need for validation becomes earning validation with our deeds. Why? Because we are conditioned to seek momentary attention/external validation as it distracts us from the cumulative impact of neglecting our foundational needs.

This avoidance magnifies our needs, making us feel as if we're too needy, our demands too big – too much. And because these needs were not met adequately by our caregivers, we subconsciously feel like we are owed. This obligation is projected onto others – they must pay for the deficit created by caregivers who were never taught the skills either. As such, we do not learn the skill of taking responsibility for ourselves. We pass this obligation on to the people around us. While the people we are in relationship with have a duty of care, it is not their job to fill the void of unmet needs – that's our job now.

When we choose ourselves and take ownership of our needs for care and support, we develop the skill of healthy independence. From this place, we can enter the realm of interdependence rather than codependence.

CHOREPLAY

Interdependence allows us to take the risk of our truth rupturing our relationships because we know we have the ability to repair and prioritize the long-term health of our relationships rather than tolerate things that could be improved. In my work as a coach, it is not uncommon for women to share that their sex lives are unsatisfying. Yet they are unable to identify what is sexually gratifying as they have not been encouraged to explore their own pleasure and sensuality. I have a workshop called 'The Potent Power of Pleasure.' Every time I deliver this workshop, women aged 40 and over share that they had not thought about their sensuality as something that belongs to them. They had always conflated their sensuality with their sexuality and believed that both were to be given away.

Furthermore, they grapple with feeling 'bad' (guilt or shame) when they consider sharing this with their long-term partner. Thus reducing their sexual pleasure to caretaking. Sometimes this is because we grow up with ideals that suggest those who love us should just be naturally attuned to our preferences. We may internalize feelings of shame about understanding and vocalizing them as society labels women who do as promiscuous. Or perhaps we are too bloody tired to enjoy sex because of all the invisible work we do! I shared this post on Instagram:

> 'Sometimes I wonder if 50 per cent of the reason why some women's libido reduces as they get older is simply because they are shattered. I think if more men contributed fairly to domestic and emotional labour, women would have the energy to be amorous. Knowing that you're not facing all of that alone is like foreplay! Your man getting home early, cooking the chicken you seasoned and putting away laundry is sexy AF. Mandem – take note!'

There were several comments supporting my proposition. One of them was sterling – 'Choreplay all day over here! It definitely lessens the brakes and boosts my sex accelerators!' – Sharon

Milone. CHOREPLAY! Someone please give Sharon an award! The consensus is that routinely unloading the dishwasher, folding and putting away laundry, sparkling surfaces, buying the ingredients for dinner, and remembering special events are the best lubricants. It is important to note that doing domestic tasks in the hope that it will lead to sex is not the same thing – that is manipulation.

Another example of why choosing you is vital. You cannot advocate for yourself in the bedroom or boardroom if you cannot identify, let alone understand, your needs or desires.

Mindful Shower

- Put a few drops of your favorite essential oil in a corner of the shower tray/bath that will get wet. Please do not put the oil where you're going to stand; although it is unlikely, you may slip. Eucalyptus, orange, and bergamot work well for uplifting and awakening. Rose, lavender, sandalwood, and frankincense are good for nurturing, soothing, and calming the nervous system.

- If you do not have these, you can use whatever essential oils you have; there is no need to buy anything in particular.

- As you wash your body, use your hands to lather the soap or shower gel on your skin. Pay attention to the way your skin feels. Focus on your skin and where your touch feels good.

- As your hands glide over parts of your body, thank them for always supporting you. As you wash your midsection (where most of our organs live), thank your organs for always doing their best for you. Thank your skin, too; it's your biggest organ, after all!

- Dry your body gently. Imagine that your skin needs the same level of tenderness as a newborn.

- As you moisturize your skin, try applying it more slowly than you usually would. Recall the type of touch that felt good in the shower and spend more time on those areas as you moisturize. For example, if you enjoyed the feel of your hands on your shoulders, mindfully moisturize that area.

//

YOUR SELF-CONCEPT MATTERS

Our self-concept is the way we see and experience ourselves. It includes our character, morals, values, skills, aspirations, and social roles. It's the template for how we relate to our inner world and the world around us. It influences the way we behave, our emotional well-being, interpersonal relationships, and even the desires we dare to dream for ourselves. Yet, this concept of self isn't formed in isolation, because we are relational creatures. Remember Ubuntu – the Southern African philosophy emphasizing communal values and interconnectedness? Our self-concept is formed by the intricate interplay of social structures around us, including the systems that oppress us.

As these structures are woven throughout the fabric of our society, they shape our internal world, skewing the prism through which we view ourselves, our worth, and our potential. For example, as we've noted previously, in a capitalist society individual worth is measured with productivity and monetary success. Consequently, those who don't, won't, or can't conform to this ideal tend to struggle with feelings of inadequacy and low self-esteem. The societal pressure to reach capitalist measures of success becomes so pervasive that it becomes internalized, subtly warping self-concept, shifting it from an innate sense of self-worth to one tethered to external measures of success.

Similarly, patriarchy creates a binary world of gender expectations, where men are conditioned to adopt 'masculine' traits such as stoicism and assertiveness. Under this system, they are forced to reject anything deemed as 'feminine' within themselves. This can lead to internalized misogyny, where they devalue and belittle 'feminine' traits, not just in women, but within themselves too. This results in stifled emotional growth and an inability to form deep, meaningful connections with themselves or others.

White supremacy implants a hierarchy of human value based on skin color into the psyche of society. This hierarchy was developed over centuries, backed by pseudo-science, the manipulation of religion, and ratified by law, creating an environment where most people of color grapple with their self-concept and have to diligently and persistently cultivate a positive identity in a society that consistently undervalues them. In such contexts, developing a robust self-concept becomes an act of resilience and defiance. I'm comforted to see a shift from Black perfection such as 'Black excellence' and 'Black girl magic,' where Black people are seen as good people as long as they are extraordinary. I'm heartened to see the mundane, ordinary, and mediocre being shared on social media platforms from 'a day in the life' videos, content under the 'Black farmer' hashtag, Black women talking about perimenopause and reclaiming their joy. I'm all the way here for the 'ordinary Black girl' and 'Black mediocrity.' Black people, people of color, and other groups that are marginalized having to be extraordinary to be accepted is oppressive. When Black people, people of color, and other groups that are marginalized are embraced for being average – for me that will be true progress!

In the context of these challenging and at times hostile environments, theories from positive psychology, such as Barbara Fredrickson's Broaden and Build theory, are a beacon of hope.[4] They demonstrate how positive emotions can help us counter these effects. Experiencing positive emotions broadens our awareness, encouraging innovative, exploratory thoughts, and actions. When applied to ourselves, this expanded thinking can lead to new knowledge, skills, outlooks, and actions helping us to build inner resources and strengthen our self-concept. The antidote to oppression is connection; fierce compassion and love are productive forces for good. The significant changes we have made as a society are born from love and care compelling people to risk their safety for the safety of others.

> *'Hate cannot drive out hate; only love can do that.'*
> **Martin Luther King, Jr.**

When considered in this way, choosing ourselves by consciously broadening positive emotions and enhancing our self-concept is not bypassing; it can become a form of joyful resistance against oppressive structures. It helps us to resist internalizing harmful stereotypes and prejudices, build resilience, and develop the boundaries necessary to challenge the status quo without sacrificing ourselves and our well-being.

I'll refer to the great Audre Lorde again: 'If I didn't define myself, I would be crunched into other people's fantasies for me and eaten alive.'

Self-Concept Reflection Exercise

This exercise is designed for you to examine your self-concept so you can recognize, understand, and name the various facets that inform your identity and self-perception.

Materials needed:

*   a notebook or journal

*   a quiet space free from distractions

*   a pen or pencil

To complete the free VIA character survey, go here: www.viacharacter.org/account/register

1. Begin by taking a moment to be present. You may want to light a candle and get some snacks so that you're able to dedicate time to this exercise. Before you start, take a deep breath and set the intention to be open throughout this exercise.

2. Write 5–10 words that come to mind when you think about yourself. They can be words you use to describe yourself, the things you do, the roles you have in life, or the things you enjoy about yourself.

3. Complete the VIA character survey and focus on the top five character strengths. See if they resonate with you and if they align with the words you used to describe yourself. Choose the five that align with you the most. You may choose two character strengths and three of the descriptors you used, or you may choose the top five character strengths, for example.

4. Elaborate on these words/strengths. Describe a recent event or a memory associated with each, noting how it impacts your life. Reflect on the positives and the challenges each presents. For example, my top strength is leadership. It means I'm good

at leading groups and encouraging them to get things done. As a challenge, it means that I usually find myself leading and find it hard to allow myself to be supported. I address this by seeking support from my leadership, having regular supervision and therapy to make sure I'm supported, and consciously putting myself in environments where I'm being led by someone else, for example, educational courses and exercise classes, and creating a protocol that helps me stop myself from taking the lead.

5. Now, think of two people in your life, a close person such as a family member or friend and one more-distant person, such as a colleague or acquaintance. How do you think these people see you? List a few descriptors for each and for extra house points, ask them! (I know; I clenched my jaw as I typed that!) Compare these to the words you've used to describe yourself.

6. Create a list of your core values and beliefs. If you're unsure of your values, you can do a free values assessment here: www.gyfted.me/quiz-landing/values-assessment

7. Consider where your values came from; for example, your upbringing, personal experiences, or cultural background. Then think about how they influence who you are and how you behave.

8. Visualize where you'd like to be five years from now. I like to imagine bumping into an old friend and updating them about how life has been over the last five years and telling them about my relationships, personal growth, career, and holistic health. If five years feels too far away, consider where you'd like to be in the next three years. Write it down. Once you have done this, look at how your description aligns or differs from your current self-concept.

Now you have completed the exercise, take a moment to reflect. Were you surprised by any of your answers? Were there areas where you felt particularly strong, or others where you'd like to change?

- Based on your reflections, outline two or three tangible steps you can take to develop your self-concept so that it reflects who you want to be.

- Look at what you said about how you'd like to be living in five years' time. How would you live from the moment you wake up to the moment you go to sleep? I invite you to start living that way now. For example, if you said you're the healthiest you've been for a long time, more energetic, doing the work you want to do, seeing your friends more often, earning more money, and happily in love, how can you start living in that now?

- In relation to your health, if you do not move your body regularly, I would invite you to do ten minutes of strenuous movement three times a week. That could be a brisk walk, shocking out to soulful house music (my preference), or Pilates. Before you dismiss the idea of ten minutes – something is better than nothing. Ten minutes three times a week for 12 weeks is 360 minutes. Because we are so adaptable, your body will adjust to this movement and begin to crave more.

- If you want to see your friends more often, my invitation would be to arrange to see your friends or invite them over for dinner and then suggest that another friend hosts a dinner in two months' time – let's be realistic, a bi-monthly is more achievable!

- If increased energy was on your list, what can you do to prioritize good quality sleep? If you have caring responsibilities, for example, small children or someone with high needs, sleep may be a challenge. If this is the case, what would be supportive for you?

- If you're a parent, what support do you need to ensure your children receive nurturing care that allows you to be a human with aspirations too? In 2022 several women in my coaching group talked about the demands of the school holidays. These women had extended family and good friends but did not ask for support as they did not want to put people out. I suggested that they look at the school calendar in advance and ask their network to support them in the holidays. These women had not thought about asking in advance and felt a sense of relief. They were also able to identify that they could do the same for their extended family and friends, too. This is an example of how choosing you helps you to choose others, too!

- Capitalism thrives on the idea of the nuclear family because it's isolating. You are confined to your immediate family unit, which means you have no choice but to consume external support. However, when we remember that we thrive in community and that our extended family and trusted friends are part of our community, we can cultivate the village required to raise a child. For me as a single parent, this meant forming relationships with two of the school mums I trusted with my child, as my daughter hated after-school club and knowing she was there and unhappy was distressing for us both. I'm forever grateful to Donna and Claire for the school pick-ups, childminding, and play dates. It also meant allowing myself to receive support from my mum, siblings, and friends. It meant consciously reminding myself that mum guilt (shame) is a product of hyper-individualism and a culture that conflates motherhood with martyrdom.

- In relation to work, how can you make your work work for you? Do you take annual leave, or do you tend to end up with lots of leave left over at the end of the year? Can you start to take planned breaks from work to do nothing? A wise use of this type of leave would be to take the day after bank holidays off, for example.

- Could you structure your workday to work with you? For example, my energy starts to wane at about 3 p.m., so I try to avoid coaching sessions at this time. It is not always possible to do this, so I'm mindful about supporting my energy for when working at this time is unavoidable. If you're an employee, this could look like telling your boss you've noticed that you're more focused in the mornings and asking that client meetings are scheduled for the afternoon.

- It could also mean starting the business you've had on your heart or restructuring your business so it works with your strengths... you may want to hire a coach to support you with this, ahem!

- We only have right now; this is where we start to experience the future. If not now, then when?

I highly recommend reviewing your self-concept quarterly to track your progress and identify patterns. Over time this will help you shift your self-concept and take aligned actions.

//

EMBODIMENT PRACTICES

Somatic practices can be powerful tools for developing a healthy self-concept, promoting well-being, and developing a deeper relationship with yourself. These practices involve re-sensitizing yourself to the sensations of your body and moving your body to support greater self-awareness, emotional regulation, and personal growth. Here are some practices to consider:

- **Yoga:** This is an ancient Indian spiritual, mental, and physical practice that integrates physical postures, breathing techniques, and meditation to promote holistic well-being. Yoga is one of the practices that allows me to meet myself, my power, and my vulnerability simultaneously. My friend and yogi Donna Noble has a mantra: 'Move your body because you love it not because you hate it.' Yoga can be a love language.

- **Tai Chi and Qi Gong:** These are traditional Chinese practices that involve slow, intentional movements combined with mindful breathing. These practices create harmony that reminds your brain that it works best in partnership with the rest of your body. I have had some of my most powerful insights during Tai Chi.

- **Strength Training:** The combination of mindful exertion, being aware of your body, and intentional movement increases physical power and mental resilience. Strenuous exercise helps to process and release stress. It increases confidence and is essential for women as we age as it helps to combat the natural loss in muscle mass and bone density, thus reducing the risk of osteoporosis. Strength training helps to support hormone health, which has been shown to have a positive impact on perimenopause symptoms. There are many more benefits to strength training – I'm a huge advocate for women lifting weights on a regular basis.

- **Mindful Walking:** Walking is a brilliant form of movement; mindfully walking is also a sign of safety. Mindful walking involves paying attention to the sensation of walking, feeling the ground beneath your feet, and having awareness of how you connect with the ground. Pay attention to how your body feels and moves with each step. This can help you ground, stay present, and feel supported. The first time I did this I was amazed at all the different sensations I felt and how good it felt to be supported by the ground. Mindful walking is one of the ways I started to feel grounded enough to 'be' inside my body without wanting to escape as soon as I felt an uncomfortable sensation.

- **Body Scan Meditation:** This is a form of meditation that involves mentally scanning each part of your body. The act of mindfully scanning your body helps you to form a connection with how you feel. It supports body awareness and can help with relaxation and stress management.

- **Breathwork:** Different breathing techniques can have various effects on your state. Deep breathing into your diaphragm can stimulate the body's relaxation response, as we tend to breathe deeper and slower when we feel safe. More vigorous breathwork practices can help your body release blocked emotions and give birth to new perspectives. My recommendation is resonant breath, as it is gentle. This involves inhaling for the count of five then pausing and then exhaling for the count of five and pausing and repeating for five minutes daily. For optimal results, it's recommended to work up to doing this for up to 20 minutes daily. I do five minutes a day as part of my morning routine as I know I can sustain this.

These practices are compassionate practices: they're not about doing it better than you did yesterday or being the best; they're an opportunity to be present. It's about learning how to listen to yourself so that you can understand and choose yourself. Over time, these somatic practices help you build a strong and trusting relationship with yourself and in turn, with your ventral vagal state. These are called practices for a reason; they need to be practiced. The regularity of your practice has a compounding effect.

GIVE YOUR TIME PURPOSE

If I had read this book eight years ago, my response would have been that this is all well and good, but I don't have time because I'm so busy. However, I'm now aware that because I was not choosing myself, I was misusing time. Learning how to partner with time enabled me to make conscious decisions so that I could be more purposeful. This has been very helpful for me as a person with 'time blindness' due to ADHD.

For people who feel like they don't have enough time, a time and motion study can be very insightful; it can also be a rude awakening. By tracking your activities and the time spent on each, you can gain a better understanding of where your time goes and identify opportunities to partner with time rather than feel like it is running away.

Believing we don't have enough time is one of the ways we embody scarcity, fueled by the urgency culture of capitalism. We have been conditioned to believe that we are constantly running out of time, as such we are perpetually anxious about time. My coaching clients often express feeling like they are behind because they should have 'it all together by now.' The feeling is so pervasive that they will feel like they are behind their agenda for the day before they get out of bed.

Time is a conduit for how we live, so when we believe we don't have enough time, unconsciously we are saying we don't have enough life. When we talk about using time effectively, we are talking about using our lives effectively. When we consider time as a conduit for life it invites a partnership where we can consider the type of relationship we want to have with our lives. For example, I want my life to feel spacious, loving, purposeful, and enjoyable, therefore I try to show up for my relationship with time in this way. I do not use time as I do not wish to be used. Instead, I partner with it by planning my time so that it supports the way I want to live as much as possible. I'm mindful about the way the language we use gives our lives meaning – working in partnership with time is powerful as opposed to being pressured by time.

To see how you're partnering with time I suggest doing a time in motion study:

- Keep a log of your daily activities for a week, noting how long you spend on each.

- Then analyze your findings: Look for patterns such as wasted time, tasks taking longer than they need to, engaging in tasks that are unimportant, and treating everything like a priority. Look at times where you're 'in flow' and seem to get more done, identify when you're more productive. Look for what precipitates these states.

Here's an example of what an average day might look like:

Time	Activity	Duration
07:00–08:00	Morning routine	1 hour
08:00–09:00	Commute to work	1 hour
09:00–13:00	Work	4 hours
13:00–14:00	Lunch	1 hour
14:00–17:00	Work	3 hours
17:00–18:00	Commute home	1 hour
18:00–20:00	Cooking, eating, clearing up	2 hours
20:00–22:30	TV, social media scrolling, messaging	2.5 hours
22:30–23:00	Bedtime routine	30 mins
23:00–07:00	Bed	8 hours

This exercise shows you how you're using your time so that you can make powerful choices about how you want to partner with time and how you'll show up for this union.

When I did this, I was able to identify a pattern of not planning my time; consequently, everything became urgent. I would then procrastinate by scrolling social media to avoid the stress of having so much to do. This was not being a good partner to time; I was not conscious about the relationship, and instead of giving it consideration and space I constantly over-filled it with busy work trying to extract every drop. This meant engaging in tasks I didn't have to or didn't want to for the sake of using my time 'well.'

I participated in a course called 'Women and Power' by an educational platform called Advaya and listened to a lecture from Riane Eisler about her 'Partnerism' framework, which is designed to shift from systems of domination to systems of partnership. This aligned with my thoughts on time and also my studies in relation to our autonomic nervous system and led me to take practical actions that enabled me to partner with the different aspects of my life, including time.

I share this as a beacon of hope if you have any feelings of shame when you do the time in motion study.

POWERFUL DECISION PROTOCOL

Looking at our relationship with time and revisiting our self-concept now that we are mindful of how we have been conditioned to see ourselves and to adapt to the world we live in brings up questions that ask us to look where we would normally look away and challenge ourselves instead of seeking the bliss of ignorance. But as we begin to understand what our nervous system is telling us, we can make conscious choices rather than be led by our unconscious patterns. To this end, I recommend creating a protocol to help you make powerful decisions.

I have strong people-pleasing tendencies and often find myself overcommitted, overstretched, and overwhelmed because I want to be 'nice,' so I ask myself these five questions before agreeing to do anything:

1. What would my response be if I prioritized being honest with myself over seeming nice?

2. How does this impact my time?

3. Bearing in mind the things I'm doing and choosing not to do, do I have the capacity for this?

4. How does this align with my intention of being a well-rested woman?

5. Will this bring me joy?

Since employing this protocol, I say no to most requests, I have changed the structure of my business, and my personal relationships are different, too. Most of all I can see how much being 'nice' was rupturing my relationship with myself, as most of the things I said yes to meant saying no to myself and constantly living outside my bandwidth and feeling like I was about to snap.

I invite you to get into the habit of asking yourself these questions before you (over)commit.

People assume they cannot do this in relation to work, as there are a number of tasks that have to be done to fulfill the job role. However, this protocol will highlight the difference between the things you need to do, the things that are the best use of your time, and the things you do habitually. A study by vouchercloud.com polled 1,989 office workers in the UK and found that on average they did two hours and 53 minutes of productive work each day, which means that on average less than half the workday is effective. So, we can begin to see how having a healthier partnership with time and making better (honest) choices is not only possible and self-affirming, but makes space for our best work, respectful, collaborative relationships, and the best fuel of all: joy.

The work of choosing you is indeed complex, messy, and uncertain. It demands a willingness to grapple with ambiguity and to tackle deep-rooted beliefs and systems that have shaped how you see yourself and experience the world. This journey requires a sense of adventure, curiosity, courage, and hope as it is likely to generate more questions than answers initially, and this is a good thing. This work requires moving at a pace that allows us to get to the heart of the matter and this means feeling what we have learned to avoid with logic. We must not resist feeling; we need to channel our attention toward feeling fully so that our commitment to growth outweighs our need for comfort.

We need to ask broad questions and wait for the answers rather than rushing to a solution for something we haven't yet understood. These questions must include, who are you at your core? This question asks you to go beyond your roles and titles. It asks you not just to consider but to declare who you are and what you need to feel emotionally and psychologically safe. Your answer will enable you to consider how you can advocate for those needs and desires so that you can take aligned action – this is not a paper exercise. This work asks us to meditate on how our needs and desires contribute to living well. Not just for our own sake, but also for the sake of a society that is committed to social justice. As we each take action in the ways that are safe and transforming for us as individuals, we each begin to create a world where our bodies and the body of the planet no longer bear the burden of feeling constantly under threat or in a state of perpetual unease. We begin to live in ways that enable our well-being to thrive, prosper, and flourish.

Joy Practice

- Think of something playful you did as a child or something playful you wanted to do as a child and schedule time to do it. My playful thing was roller-skating, which I resumed in 2016. For me, roller-skating was freedom and joy and I still get that feeling when I skate now.

- As children, my cousins and I used to watch an Indian film called 'Pinky and Suki' (it might not have been called that, but that's what we called it). We were obsessed with the singing and dancing; I loved the way the women moved their midriffs and moved their hands. This memory led me to belly dance classes. I know that belly dancing isn't the same, but it gives me so much joy and provides me with an embodied experience of what it is to learn something new.

- If you're stuck for ideas, have a look at what your local college has to offer. Many of them have a range of low-cost activities.

//

Dear One,

You are the prize and the entire celebration.

So distinguishable there will only ever be one you.

Your presence is the manifestation of
your ancestors' wildest imagination.

Please don't take their dreams for granted.

Your life will be a DNA expression for future
generations via the fruit of your loins or
your contribution to our systems.

You're not a work in progress, you are progress.
A living testament to resilience and hope.

It's time to stop proving yourself so
you can finally be yourself.

Never forget that you are a miracle.

CHAPTER 9

CREATE YOUR LIFE MANIFESTO

'Dangerous is the woman who can give herself what she used to seek from others. Limitless is the woman who dares to name herself.'

Tarana Burke

We simply cannot continue to (over)function as we are. It's time to break free from toxic productivity and find our joy!

Capitalism is degenerative. It zaps your life-force energy by corroding your well-being so you're malnourished; therefore, regenerative self-care must be non-negotiable. I'm not talking about bubble baths, occasional retreats, and exercise that feels like corporal punishment. I'm talking about deep and nourishing self-care at a core level that enables you to rebuild your foundation. From tending to your needs and creating a strong self-concept to healthy boundaries and allowing yourself to want what you want because you want it. Regenerative self-care requires introspection, compassion, and an unwavering commitment to actively engaging in regulating practices and habits that nourish your body, mind, and soul.

Capitalism thrives on your dysregulation and distraction. Nourished women who are in charge of their attention are a threat because we don't merely survive – we choose to live, love, and work with intention.

When you're emotionally, mentally, physically, and spiritually malnourished, you'll preoccupy yourself with arbitrary goals that steal your soul. This behavior leaves a void that you have been conditioned to fill by commodifying yourself – we are conditioned to consume what is actually innate. For example, mental malnourishment is met with overload because we mistake peace for boredom and try to counter it by overstimulating ourselves with information. Physical malnourishment is met with grueling workouts at expensive gyms, fancy supplements in place of nourishing foods, and hacks and fads aimed to help us 'optimize' when what we need is nurturing care. Spiritual malnourishment is met with appropriation, false humility, and transactions to help us get what we want rather than genuine inner development and understanding so we can be who we truly are.

So, what does regenerative self-care look like in practice?

• When we choose to nourish ourselves deeply and live with intention, we not only reclaim our agency, but we also model a more harmonious way of living, and we have the temerity to demand change to facilitate collective healing and liberation. It's a radical act of love.

• Before we rush headfirst into creating solutions that stifle, we will cultivate a level of inner safety that radiates outward, promoting a culture of care, belonging, and connection. This will create a nourishing environment that is not seduced by busyness, instead supporting the stillness and space necessary to hear with our hearts, feel with our intuition, and see with compassionate eyes.

• With this compassion, we can look at our anger as it points to injustice, instead of making ourselves wrong for having a human reaction to what is inhumane. As we do this, we will heal the shame of our internalized conditioning so we may divest from false order and negative peace, enabling us to move toward positive peace and the presence of justice. We must bear the heat of unlearning so we can reach the temperate climate needed to foster meaningful connections rather than settle for lukewarm acceptance.

- We will not shrink. We will not hide. We will not over-function. We will care for ourselves without condition and create conditions that allow us to care for others without compromising who we are and what we need to be whole. We will tend to sorrow so it may tenderize, opening us to the soul work of being present with the unknown until it becomes known.

- This undertaking will ruffle feathers, confuse, and possibly garner judgment from those who benefited from us being trapped in a pervasive sense of low self-worth and dysregulation we tried to please our way out of. We must not let their projection stain our reflection.

- We shall remember the trinity of oppression has been in place for centuries. Therefore, we will not set ourselves up to fail with impossible timescales. Instead, we will acknowledge that we may be planting seeds that will blossom in another lifetime and we will be at peace knowing this is the work of legacy, shifting the trajectory of species and planet.

- We must be prepared to let others be wrong about us. It is safer for us to be wrong in the minds of others than to be wrong in our own. We will make the most gracious assumptions about ourselves, treating ourselves with the compassion we would extend to a dear friend. We will not self-abandon.

- May we reclaim ourselves and each other so we experience what it is to be whole. May we commit to filling ourselves with unconditional love so we can love others from the bounty of overflow.

- We must not allow the limitations of others to become limitations of our own. We must declare that it is not just safe for us to want what we want and go for it with vigor – it is imperative. Our well-being depends on it. We must accept that anyone who is threatened by us living our richest lives because we no longer conform to the role they have assigned us is not actually for us. Although agonizing, it's not as painful as the torment of self-abandonment for the false perception of another. It is safer to rupture relationships with people and systems than to rupture your relationship with yourself.

- We must be willing to choose the finite, intense pain of change instead of succumbing to the temporary relief of convenience followed by the pervasive, dull ache of conformity.

- We must be prepared to make mistakes and let go of the childlike need to look like a 'good girl' and choose to be bold women instead. From this place of maturity, we can rebuild and renew. We commit to self-compassion over chastisement and courage over fear, so our bodies may become safe havens where our nervous systems can rest. From this place of belonging, we can appreciate how interconnected we are – individuals coming together to form one movement.

- May we be fortified with a love for self, the planet, and each other that enables us to say a wholehearted, sensual YES to life.

- We are no longer willing to lean in and replicate oppression disguised as equality in a slick pantsuit or midi-dress and trainers. We will stand for equity and sit for rest as a reclamation of ourselves, liberation from toxic productivity, and a commitment to our divinity. We will not be martyrs. We will be well rested, deeply connected, and powerFULL.

CREATE YOUR LIFE MANIFESTO

I often invite my clients to create a manifesto. A manifesto is a document where you share your beliefs, goals, and intentions. It can be a north star, pointing you in the direction of your values and aspirations. A manifesto can also be a beautiful reminder of who you are and what you stand for, which is vital when you commit to transformation. Survival patterns run deep, therefore nurturing ourselves needs practice and reminders.

I'm going to invite you to create your own manifesto to be the north star for your transformation. Before that, I would like to share this reminder.

1. It's Not Your Fault

You did not choose the conditioning that shaped your understanding of the world, but you can create new conditions for yourself and others. In a world that has reduced you to what you can do for others, choosing yourself and your joy is a healing balm that allows your authenticity to shine.

2. You Had to Adapt

Toxic-productivity culture tells you that your worth is tethered to your output. As such, you adapted as a means of survival, but now you know that you cannot survive and thrive. You are not a commodity to be extracted from; you're a living, breathing, sentient being with emotion, passion, and depth. In choosing to thrive, you choose to rediscover yourself.

3. You Are Your Nervous System's Best Friend

By learning how to be your nervous system's best friend, you can make choices that support you from a place of safety rather than your conditioning. This is essential as you do the work of breaking free from toxic productivity and finding your joy. Joy can feel like a threat to a nervous system that is not used to it. Knowing your nervous system gives you the power to build trust so your body learns how to hold joy.

4. Be the Real You

Oppression dims your light. However, meeting the real you helps you become radiant as you forgive yourself for not knowing what you didn't know and find joy in your identity, culture, and history. In meeting the real you, you begin to outshine the shadows of systems that hold you back.

5. We Are Naturally Productive

We have a natural capacity to produce and create. Our productivity can support us to create a meaningful life where we have time to work, rest, and enjoy. In embracing what is innate, we can choose meaningful aspirations over arbitrary goals and prioritize people and planet over profit.

6. Know Your Bandwidth

Your bandwidth is a sacred space that allows you to make informed choices about how you use your life-force energy. It tells you what you need and when you need it. It is a wellspring of information about you. Listening to your bandwidth helps you to unshackle yourself from metrics made for machines and trust your own innate wisdom.

7. Relationships Are a Revolution

The antidote to oppression is connection and belonging, the true genius of our species. Developing the skill of vulnerability enables you to engage in relationships where you're truly known. In being true to yourself and your relationships, you set a precedent. Women are not naturally competitive; we are collaborative, and in this collaboration, we will find joy and freedom.

8. Choosing You Is Essential

Choosing you isn't selfish. It's your salvation. It teaches you how to resource yourself so that you do not outsource yourself to ever-moving targets and systems that rely on your exhaustion. You are worthy of nourishing relationships and leadership that is just, but you must demand it of yourself and others as it will not be given freely.

You are not alone in this journey; women all over the world are rising up. It's time to let go of that inherited conditioning and reclaim your story. Stand tall in your authenticity, look beyond the toxic busyness, and recognize the vibrant, multifaceted being you are.

Choose yourself. Every. Single. Time. Why? Because doing so is not just an act of personal redemption, it's a revolutionary stance for the collective.

[Name's] Manifesto for Joyful Living

What I Stand For

Affirmation: State in one powerful sentence what you stand for.

Example: I stand for integrity, empathy, justice, and revolutionary love.

My Core Beliefs

Statement: Identify your most cherished beliefs.

Example: I believe in the power of connection and belonging and the transformative power of compassion. I know that social justice is necessary for us to create a system that cares for all its citizens.

My Values

Declaration: List your top three values.

Example: Authenticity, courage, compassion.

My Life Commitment

Commitment: State how you choose to live your life.

Example: I commit to living a life of intention, where I consciously choose to honor myself, uplift others, and treat our planet with reverence.

Unlearning My Conditioning

Promise: Describe how you'll commit to unlearning societal or self-imposed limitations.

Example: I promise to question the narratives that limit my potential and to replace them with empowering truths.

Defining Myself

Definition: State how you choose to define yourself.

Example: I define myself by living according to my values and allowing my strengths to shine.

My Gifts and Talents

Acknowledgment: List your gifts and talents that can enrich your life and that of others.

Example: I acknowledge my gift for empathetic listening and my talent for creative solutions.

For The Community and Against Injustice

Pledge: Describe how you'll contribute to community well-being and stand against injustice.

Example: I commit to using my voice and actions to support marginalized communities and challenge systems of oppression.

Prioritizing Joy and Radical Self-Care

Intention: State how you'll prioritize joy and self-care.

Example: I will make space for joy by scheduling time to engage in activities that nourish my soul, and by practicing radical self-care.

Dealing with Setbacks and Hardships

Resilience: Describe your approach to handling life's difficulties.

Example: When faced with setbacks, I will remember that each challenge is an opportunity for growth and lean in to my support network. I do not have to handle challenges alone.

Grace in Mistakes

Forgiveness: State how you'll treat yourself after making mistakes.

Example: I will meet mistakes with understanding and forgiveness, seeing them as lessons rather than a condemnation of my character.

Being Over Doing

Humanity: Describe how you'll allow yourself to be a human being rather than a productivity machine.

Example: I give myself permission to be, not just to do; to value rest, reflection, and the journey as much as accomplishments.

The Courage to Let Go

Courage: Explain how you'll muster the courage to leave behind people and situations that don't serve you.

Example: I will have the courage to distance myself from relationships and situations that don't honor my authenticity so I may create space for aligned relationships.

No More Neglect

Self-Love: State how you'll ensure you never neglect your needs.

Example: I commit to listening to my nervous system states and remember that my needs are a bid for connection. I know that when I honor them, I honor me and heal the wounds of the past.

Words to Live By

Quote: Share a powerful quote that resonates with your journey.

Example: "It's time to update the narrative about you according to the growth and evolution that has made you who you are now." – Dawn Estefan, Psychotherapist

//

Once you have completed the manifesto you can remove the headings so that it reads smoothly. You do not have to write sentences; you can write paragraphs if you choose. However, try to keep it concise as this is a document I encourage you to read often. How often is often? That is for you to decide. I used to read mine daily. Now I read it whenever I remember.

This is your manifesto; it is designed to be an empowering document for life. Adapt it as you evolve, and let it guide you in moments of doubt or need. It is a reminder of who you are, what you stand for, and your ability to effect change in your world and the world. Let this document be your anchor. I recommend doing this on a Google doc or similar, as all your changes will be recorded and you'll be able to reflect on previous versions and see how you evolve. I suggest reviewing your manifesto each birthday.

CONCLUSION

In June 2023 I was hosting an online quarterly planning day with my coaching clients. I often sit at my living room window during video calls. The lighting is beautiful, which is advantageous when you're on a video screen. Also, I like the view from my window. There are trees that always look appealing to my eyes and provide a co-regulation pause. Being able to take momentary eye breaks to savor the view from my window invites me to soften into the moment and be present, rather than fatigued from staring at a screen.

We were approaching our lunch break; as I looked at the screen to tell the women we were about to pause I was struck by the fact that I was looking at the type of women I dreamed about supporting when I transitioned from my social work career to my coaching business. At the same time, I noticed my daughter walking through the garden gate. Our eyes met. We instantly smiled and I gave her a little wave.

I returned to the screen, acknowledged the women for the work we had done during the first part of our day, and ended the morning's proceedings.

I paused the video recording, turned my camera off, put my laptop on mute, and greeted my daughter at the top of the stairs. We had a conversation about the exam she had just taken whilst I made us lunch. After lunch my daughter went into her bedroom to continue studying for her GCSE exams and I to my video call for the second half of the quarterly planning day.

Whilst I was on the call, my daughter sent a message asking if she could meet her friends in the park. I agreed and waved at her from the window as she set off. When the quarterly planning day ended, I had a short debrief as I normally do to reflect on what went well, what I would do differently, and to celebrate myself.

As I began to write about what I was celebrating I felt warm ripples from my lower abdomen flowing toward my heart and throat. It almost felt overwhelming; I felt my breath becoming shallow and my heart rate increasing. My automatic reaction was to try and shut my feelings down by doing something else. I stopped myself as I remembered that my sensations are messengers, not threats. I inhaled deeply and as I exhaled, I allowed myself to feel those warm waves. As I felt the ripples tears started to flow; it didn't feel like I was crying, it felt like some of my 'freeze' was thawing.

In that moment, I was at one with the fact that I was living the life I vowed I would live when I was crying in my boss's office in January 2009. I understood that those tears were stewardship from my body guiding me to make powerful choices; rather than a sign of weakness or that I couldn't cope, they were flagging that something needed to change. My panic attack on the way to court in September 2017 was a rallying cry from my body demanding a system overhaul.

As the tears flowed I reflected on the quarterly planning day, and I understood that these tears were tears of joy, a gentle release for finally listening to the wisdom of my body, even when it went against the grain of my conditioning. I imagined my grandmothers and their grandmothers experiencing this moment with me through their imprint on my DNA. I felt release, relief, and power.

I felt the release of grief for all the things I had missed as an overworked social worker who was working far too much and experiencing far too little joy. I felt relief that the risks I had taken were not in vain; my actions facilitated a transformation that benefits me and has enabled me to have more energy for my child.

I felt power because I had been able to do what I thought was impossible – I created impactful work that works for me, too. And in terms of my personal relationships, I learned that I have the right to have boundaries that support connection and belonging. Whilst this means that some relationships have had to become more distant, it means that some have become richer.

The work to get to this point has been excruciating at times, but not as excruciating as it was to endure an existence that relied on me abandoning myself. The friendship with my nervous system had truly begun.

Please note, I said 'begun'! I'll always be in toxic-productivity recovery. The allure of organizing my existence around working too much still enchants me and there are many times when I slip into my over-functioning ways. The difference now is that I meet myself with compassion and support myself with grounding techniques that remind me I'm holy.

This is the compounding effect of the *gradual* changes I made day after day. There was no singular event – it was meeting myself with compassion and connecting with my needs over and over and over again, especially when I wanted to shut my needs up.

Capitalism tells us that change should be fast, intense, and yield immediate results. Embodied wisdom tells us that trust and meaningful change require time, repetition, and care.

Here I am, a dark-skinned Black African woman, a daughter of immigrants creating a life that feels regenerative because I have dared to tend to my needs, create healthy boundaries, and get clear about who I am and whose I am. I stand tall on a sturdy foundation backed by intergenerational resilience and growth. I continue to do the work to understand what satisfies me and to own my desires. Contrary to white-supremacist stereotypes, I'm learning to appreciate being soft. I recognize that my fragility is the key to my strength and remember to trust that is safe for me to walk away from people, places, and spaces that rely on me denying my reality. There is no opportunity that is worth denying my truth. In Sierra Leone there is a saying, 'Water that is for you will never run past you.' This I know to be true.

In 2017 actress Tracee Ellis Ross gave a keynote speech at the *Glamour* magazine's women of the year summit. The video of the speech on *Glamour*'s website is called 'Tracee Ellis Ross Is Living For Herself.'[1] The speech went viral. The part of the speech that has stayed with me is when she said, 'My life is mine. My life is mine.' In 2017, as I was experiencing an existential crisis, my life did not feel like it was mine. It felt like a high-speed runaway train being driven by the patriarchy. Learning how to be a friend to my nervous system has put me back in the driving seat so I can determine the speed, journey, and destination.

My life is mine.

Over the course of this book, I have set out the ways in which the trinity of oppression seeps into our everyday lives, keeping us in a state of survival, so that you can see how much of your life has been dominated by these oppressive forces.

It is a wake-up call.

But before you rush into doing and turn being a friend to your nervous system, a job on your to-do list: I invite you to listen inward so you can hear yourself.

You are not a work-in-progress who must work on her mindset to overcome self-limiting beliefs. Most of these perceived limitations are an outcome of systemic oppression. To break free from toxic productivity, we must understand what created the environment that normalized chronic overwork as a means for women to prove their worth. And we must understand the way this phenomenon is exacerbated where womanhood intersects with race. The antidote to the trinity of oppression is connection, belonging, and compassion, and these things are only true if they are intersectional.

SO WHAT NOW?

The main reason I have been able to transform my experience is because I have consciously chosen to put myself in expansive spaces with like-minded women on a similar journey. When those spaces have not been available, I have created them.

This is not a solo endeavor. We begin the task of listening by listening to ourselves and each other. Therefore, now that you have read this book, I suggest reading it again in community with like-minded people so you can explore the topics together. I encourage you to engage in thought partnership so that you and others can think about the content of this book together and play with your thoughts like a Rubik's Cube. See how the combinations you create test ways you can solve parts of the puzzle.

I invite you to be courageous and bold. This could look like reaching out to your faves on social media and inviting them to be part of your thought partnership via video call or voice note messages.

I'll be even folder and invite you to join my membership group, The Life & Business Sanctuary. It is an education and networking platform for socially conscious, values-driven women in business and leadership. A recent masterclass and discussion was called 'The Patriarchy Doesn't Want You To Make Cute Money, But I Do.' We discussed how we have internalized the patriarchy, how it limits growth and collaboration, and explored how we can address this. Despite the heaviness of the topic, we were able to have a powerful conversation that led to us all committing to making choices and being the change we want to see. We didn't catastrophize, we strategized. And we were able to do this because we did it together. There truly is strength in numbers.

The exercises and Joy practices throughout this book may appear to be small drops in an ocean. However, with repetition and devotion they can create significant ripples. If you amplify them in community, these ripples become huge waves. On that note, I invite you to engage in some of the activities with your friends or like-minded peers; for example, a monthly communal self-care Sunday practice with your friends via video, where you do one or two of the practices together.

The oppressive trinity thrives on your silence and isolation. I'm inviting you to rebel against this with acts of radical self-love, community care, and social justice.

ENDNOTES

Chapter 1: How Did We Get Here?

1. van der Kolk, B. (2015), *The Body Keeps the Score: Brain, Mind, and Body in the Healing of Trauma.* New York: Penguin Books.

2. Maté, G. (2018), *In the Realm of Hungry Ghosts: Close Encounters with Addiction.* London: Vermilion.

3. No doubt a reference to Gilroy, P. (1991), *There Ain't No Black in the Union Jack: The Cultural Politics of Race and Nation.* Chicago: University of Chicago Press.

4. Departmental News (2019), 'Burn-out an "occupational phenomenon": International Classification of Diseases': www.who.int/news/item/28-05-2019-burn-out-an-occupational-phenomenon-international-classification-of-diseases [Accessed 28 August 2023].

5. McRae, K., et al. (2008), 'Gender Differences in Emotion Regulation: An fMRI study of cognitive reappraisal', *Group Process Intergroup Relat*, 11(2): 143–162.

6. Demby, G. (2018), 'Making the Case That Discrimination Is Bad For Your Health': www.npr.org/sections/codeswitch/2018/01/14/577664626/making-the-case-that-discrimination-is-bad-for-your-health [Accessed 28 August 2023].

7. Hanson, R., 'Take in the Good' exercise: https://www.rickhanson.net/take-in-the-good/ [Accessed 28 August 2023].

Chapter 2: How You Have (Mal)adapted

1. Descartes, R. (1998), *Meditations and Other Metaphysical Writings*. London: Penguin Classics.

2. Tan, S.Y., et al. (2018), 'Founder of the Stress Theory', *Singapore Med,* 59(4): 170–171.

3. Maslow, A.H. (1943), 'A Theory of Human Motivation', *Psychological Review*, 50(4): 370–396.

4. World Health Organization (2023), 'Air pollution: The Invisible Health Threat': www.who.int/news-room/feature-stories/detail/air-pollution–the-invisible-health-threat [Accessed 28 August 2023].

5. Walker, P., 'The 4Fs: A Trauma Typology in Complex PTSD': www.pete-walker.com/fourFs_TraumaTypologyComplexPTSD.htm [Accessed 28 August 2023].

6. Kim, S., Kim, J. (2007), 'Mood After Various Brief Exercise and Sport Modes: Aerobics, Hip-hop Dancing, Ice Skating, and Body Conditioning', *Percept Mot Skills*, 104(3 Pt 2):1265–70.

7. Newman, K.M. (2022), 'Four Ways Dancing Makes You Happier', *Greater Good Magazine*: greatergood.berkeley.

edu/article/item/four_ways_dancing_makes_you_happier
[Accessed 28 August 2023].

Chapter 3: Be Your Nervous System's Best Friend

1. Brown, B. (2010), 'The power of vulnerability': www.ted.com/
talks/brene_brown_the_power_of_vulnerability [Accessed
28 August 2023].

2. Brown, B. (2020), *The Gifts of Imperfection*. London:
Vermilion.

3. Gordon, B. (2014), 'Your Mind Does Not Care What Your
Brain Thinks': www.psychologytoday.com/gb/blog/obesely-
speaking/
201403/your-mind-does-not-care-what-your-brain-thinks
[Accessed 28 August 2023].

4. Theopedia: https://www.theopedia.com/joy [Accessed
28 August 2023].

5. Maurer, Roy. (2020), 'New DE&I Roles Spike After Racial
Justice Protests': www.shrm.org/resourcesandtools/hr-topics/
talent-acquisition/pages/new-dei-roles-spike-after-racial-justice-
protests.aspx [Accessed 26 October 2023].

6. Bunn, C. (2023), 'Hamstrung by 'golden handcuffs': Diversity
roles disappear 3 years after George Floyd's murder
inspired them': www.nbcnews.com/news/nbcblk/diversity-
roles-disappear-three-years-george-floyd-protests-inspired-
rcna72026 [Accessed 28 August 2023].

7. Donnelly, L. (2022), 'NHS to cut diversity and inclusion jobs in
management shakeup': www.telegraph.co.uk/news/2022/06/

08/nhs-cut-diversity-inclusion-jobs-management-shakeup/ [Accessed 28 August 2023].

8. Porges, S. 'Polyvagal Theory': www.stephenporges.com [Accessed 28 August 2023].

Chapter 4: Meeting the Real You

1. The Centers for Disease Control and Prevention (CDC): www.cdc.gov/genomics/disease/epigenetics.htm. [Accessed 27 September 2023].

2. Sumioka, H. et al. (2013), 'Huggable communication medium decreases cortisol levels': www.ncbi.nlm.nih.gov/pmc/articles/ PMC3805974/ [Accessed 28 August 2023].

3. Neff, K. (2011), *Self-Compassion*. London: Yellow Kite.

Chapter 5: Be Naturally Productive

1. Moore, E. (2019), *Dream Yourself Free: A Workbook for Womanist Healing, Dreaming, and Purpose Building*.

2. Carr, M. (2023), 'The Motherhood Penalty': www.henley.ac.uk/ news/2023/the-motherhood-penalty [Accessed 27 September 2023].

3. Equality and Human Rights Commission (2015): www. equalityhumanrights.com/en/our-work/news/pregnancy-and-maternity-discrimination-forces-thousands-new-mothers-out-their-jobs [Accessed 27 September 2023].

4. Hochschild, A. (2012), *The Second Shift: Working Families and the Revolution at Home*. New York: Penguin.

5. OECD Statistics, 'Average usual weekly hours worked on the main job': stats.oecd.org/Index.aspx?DataSetCode=AVE_HRS [Accessed 27 September 2023].

6. Broom, D. (2019), 'Why Nordic nations are the best places to have children': www.weforum.org/agenda/2019/03/nordic-nations-best-places-for-parents-children/ [Accessed 27 September 2023].

7. Rock, L. (2012), 'What Britain could learn from Denmark's childcare model': www.theguardian.com/society/2012/feb/18/britain-learn-denmark-childcare-model [Accessed 27 September 2023].

8. Dictionary.com: www.dictionary.com/browse/best [Accessed 27 September 2023].

9. Möller-Levet, C., et al. (2013), 'Effects of insufficient sleep on circadian rhythmicity and expression amplitude of the human blood transcriptome', *PNAS*, 110(12): E1132–E1141.

10. Duffy, J.F., et al. (2011), 'Sex difference in the near-24-hour intrinsic period of the human circadian timing system', *PNAS*, 108(3): 15602–15608.

11. Williamson, M. (2015), *A Return to Love*. London: Harper Thorsons.

Chapter 6: Know Your Bandwidth

1. Kübler-Ross, E. (2008), *On Death and Dying: What the Dying have to teach Doctors, Nurses, Clergy and their own Families*. Oxford: Routledge.

2. UCL Berkeley, 'What are personal boundaries?': uhs.berkeley.edu/sites/default/files/relationships_personal_boundaries.pdf [Accessed 28 August 2023]

3. Dalton-Smith, S. (2019), *Sacred Rest*. Nashville: FaithWords.

4. Seppala, E. (2017), *The Happiness Track: How to apply the science of happiness to accelerate your success.* London: HarperOne.

5. Williamson, M. (2015), *A Return to Love*. London: Harper Thorsons.

Chapter 7: Relationships Are Revolutionary

1. Blumenfeld, R. (2020), 'How A 15,000-Year-Old Human Bone Could Help You Through The Coronacrisis': www.forbes.com/sites/remyblumenfeld/2020/03/21/how-a-15000-year-old-human-bone-could-help-you-through-the–coronavirus/ [Accessed 27 September 2023].

2. Fraser, N., et al. (2019), *Feminism for the 99%: A Manifesto.* London: Verso Books.

3. The Priory, 'Why Are Suicides So High Amongst Men?': https://www.priorygroup.com/blog/why-are-suicides-so-high-amongst-men [Accessed 27 September 2023].

Chapter 8: Choosing You

1. Lorde, A. (1988), *A Burst of Light: and Other Essays*. Ithaca, NY: Firebrand Books.

2. McKinsey & Company (2022), 'Women in the Workplace': www.mckinsey.com/~/media/mckinsey/featured%20insights/

diversity%20and%20inclusion/women%20in%20the%20
workplace%202022/women-in-the-workplace-2022.pdf
[Accessed 28 August 2023].

3. Morrison said this in an interview with broadcaster Charlie
Rose on the Charlie Rose show in 1993.

4. Fredrickson, B. (2011), *Positivity: Groundbreaking Research
to Release Your Inner Optimist And Thrive*. London:
Oneworld Publications.

Conclusion

1. Ellis Ross, T. (2017), 'Tracee Ellis Ross Is Living For Herself':
www.glamour.com/video/watch/tracee-ellis-ross-is-living-for-
herself [Accessed on 24 September 2023].

RESOURCES

MEDITATIONS

You can listen to recordings of some of the meditations featured in the book at womenwhoworktoomuch.co. They, as well as all other meditations, can also be found in the audiobook, which is available in the *Empower You Unlimited Audio* app or wherever you listen to your audiobooks.

COURSES AND COACHING

Advaya

Women and Power

www.advaya.co/events/series/women-and-power

Deb Dana

The Foundations of Polyvagal Informed Practice

www.rhythmofregulation.com/foundations

Nicola Rae

A Life More Inspired

www.alifemoreinspired.com

ACKNOWLEDGMENTS

Firstly, in the words of Snoop Dogg, I would like to thank me for being me!

I would also like to thank Emine Rushton for giving me the opportunity to write a column for *Oh* magazine; this was the beginning of this book's journey. Thank you for reading so many of my mini blogs on Instagram and giving me a bigger space to share my thoughts in print. This column is where my agent read my words and approached me about writing a book.

Thank you Valeria Huerta, the best agent in town and my unofficial Bolivian Aunty. Thank you for seeing me and for your patience; you've had my back throughout and I appreciate you. Your wise counsel, negotiation skills, and enthusiasm for me and my work have felt so supportive.

Cara Conquest – you're a testament to the power of connection. Thank you for telling Pippa to check me out on social media; without your recommendation this would not be my first book! Clearly the Divine had other plans and made you one of my angel guides; thank you is the tip of the iceberg.

Pippa Wright, without you sliding into my Instagram DMs I would not have realized that I was banging on about toxic productivity! Your message sent me down the rabbit hole of my own content and helped me see that I had always been talking about it in one way, shape, or form. I cannot thank you enough. Without your interest I would have been writing a book about everyday joy in midlife, which is cool and may still come. However, toxic productivity feels like my calling.

A special thank you to Helen Rochester and the team at Hay House UK – my goodness, you have been utterly wonderful. If Carlsberg made book publishing experiences, this would be it. You have handled me and this project with a level of care and support that has felt breathtaking at times. I remember walking into the conference room at Hay House and feeling like I was living a dream. I had heard tales of other Black women's publishing journeys and was prepared for an uphill climb, but you provided me with the gentlest landing place. From our initial meeting, I have felt valued.

Kate Adams, what can I say? Thank you for getting it and getting me. Hearing you say, 'This is activism' was such a relief, I knew my words would be in safe hands. Thank you for being such a wonderful book doula, and always meeting me where I was with kindness and a boost when I felt like I was wading through treacle. The way you were gave my many, many words containment and felt like a relief. Thank you for being like a lighthouse guiding me back to shore.

Vimbai Shire, your words have felt like prayers and affirmations and so did your editing. I'm delighted that Hay House asked you to edit my book and that you were available. Your understanding of the nuances and your ability to cut through to the heart of the story and weave it together seamlessly made the editing process feel smooth.

My Zia Booms, thank you for being such a brilliant sounding board and for helping me with my Dear Ones. Writing this book whilst you're at an age where you can listen to me, read my work, and give me feedback has felt like a precious gift. I hope this journey and these words help you avoid the trap of over-working to prove your worth. Never forget: you are Earth and Heaven in human form. I love you more than words could ever articulate.

Elijah Sam, sometimes when I got stuck, I would listen to your voice notes because they always make me feel ventral.

Big shout out to my cousin Mariam for giving me tips to help me focus, along with phone calls and messages to check up on me. Thank goodness you didn't get taken away by the boogie man when you went off on that train!!!

Mus and Vanessa, your cheerleading, pride, and words of encouragement were like a healing balm; you defo have mum's cheerleader gene!

Dawn Estefan, your therapy grounds me like Mother Earth, hydrates me like the first water, breathes air like sea breeze, and lights a fire in my heart that reminds me that I can – especially if I feel. Thank you.

Aunty Aminatta, you are one of the most inspiring women I have ever known. You had such an impact on me. On the surface, it seemed so small but the way you carried yourself and what looked like your exuberance made a massive imprint on my heart. I think you were my first conscious role model.

Mum, my ultimate inspiration, cheerleader, and guide. You have taught me to back myself and always look for something of beauty and value no matter how small. Your faith in God, life, and yourself has allowed me to know that I will always overcome. Having you to bounce ideas off and explore my curiosities is a gift, and I appreciate the way you have no doubt in me and my aspirations. You always provide the words and support to fuel my ambitions, as well as the love and care to remind me to slow down and enjoy the journey.

My wonderful friends, thank you for celebrating me and cheering me on: Neena, Wanita, Rose, Leah R, Andrea, Kelly, Leanna, Sharon, Ray, Selina, Chioma, Sareta, Yvadney, Lizzie.

Leah Samuel and Nicola Rae – you have been like shining stars helping me chart the way. I cherish your friendship.

NangNeenaWoy, you are a total cherub, thank you for reading (promptly), listening intently, and being so encouraging.

Emma Innes, the best English tutor in the world, thank you for your energy, expertise, and care.

A very big shout out to the women who have been part of my Sovereign program – our work together informed this book and the way I work. Massive shout out to Maki for helping me trust that in a world of fast-paced everything, my work is an opportunity to go slowly, go gently, go powerfully.

Donna Noble – I cannot thank you enough for your writing advice – just write, don't write and edit, remember the first draft is the first draft – what a relief!

My Dawn Writers!!! Jade, Donna, Karen, Ellen, Sas, Gem Gems, and Katty – thank you for that early hour; your company was instrumental.

A huge great big thank you to the teachers who have taught me so much and informed the way I live and work. Nathan Blair, you and The Somatic School changed my life and my business. Nathan, what you have created is a gift to humanity. I'll forever be grateful for somatic coach training with you. Steve Hoskinson, Organic Intelligence® needs to be taught in schools. Deb Dana and the Polyvagal Informed Practice team, your work has shaped how I do things. Micheala Boehm, thank you for your teaching; your Non-Linear Movement Method training helped me experience embodiment.

Vickie Remoe, thank you for allowing me to share part of your story. Thank you for tirelessly working to improve the experience of life in Sierra Leone and for being a supportive friend. I appreciate you.

And lastly to my GG's, my good grandparents – especially my Granddad Rufai Moses Richardson Thomas, who was by my side every step of the way.

Photo by Bry Penney

ABOUT THE AUTHOR

Tamu Thomas is a transformational coach, writer, workshop facilitator, podcaster, and somatic movement practitioner.

A former social worker, she set up her values-driven coaching business Live Three Sixty to help over-functioning, over-working, high-achieving women to live and work more authentically, establish boundaries, find their purpose, and make good money. She has been featured in *Vogue*, *Forbes*, ITV, *Women & Home*, *Bustle*, *Adulting with Ebonie*, and others.

 livethreesixty.com

 LIVE-THREE-SIXTY

 livethreesixty

 livethreesixty_

We hope you enjoyed this Hay House book. If you'd like to receive our online catalog featuring additional information on Hay House books and products, or if you'd like to find out more about the Hay Foundation, please contact:

Hay House, Inc., P.O. Box 5100, Carlsbad, CA 92018-5100
(760) 431-7695 or (800) 654-5126
(760) 431-6948 (fax) or (800) 650-5115 (fax)
www.hayhouse.com® • www.hayfoundation.org

———

Published in Australia by: Hay House Australia Pty. Ltd.,
18/36 Ralph St., Alexandria NSW 2015
Phone: 612-9669-4299 • *Fax:* 612-9669-4144
www.hayhouse.com.au

Published in the United Kingdom by: Hay House UK, Ltd.,
The Sixth Floor, Watson House, 54 Baker Street, London W1U 7BU
Phone: +44 (0)20 3927 7290 • *Fax:* +44 (0)20 3927 7291
www.hayhouse.co.uk

Published in India by: Hay House Publishers India,
Muskaan Complex, Plot No. 3, B-2, Vasant Kunj, New Delhi 110 070
Phone: 91-11-4176-1620 • *Fax:* 91-11-4176-1630
www.hayhouse.co.in

———

Access New Knowledge.
Anytime. Anywhere.

Learn and evolve at your own pace
with the world's leading experts.

www.hayhouseU.com

CONNECT WITH
HAY HOUSE
ONLINE

🌐 hayhouse.co.uk   **f** @hayhouse

📷 @hayhouseuk   𝕏 @hayhouseuk

▶ @hayhouseuk   ♪ @hayhouseuk

Find out all about our latest books & card decks • Be the first to know about exclusive discounts • Interact with our authors in live broadcasts • Celebrate the cycle of the seasons with us • Watch free videos from your favourite authors • Connect with like-minded souls

'The gateways to wisdom and knowledge are always open.'

Louise Hay